Successful Science Teaching

Improving achievement and learning engagement by using classroom assessment

Paul Spenceley

With a foreword by
Dylan Wiliam

First published 2022

by John Catt Educational Ltd,
15 Riduna Park, Station Road,
Melton, Woodbridge IP12 1QT

Tel: +44 (0) 1394 389850
Fax: +44 (0) 1394 386893
Email: enquiries@johncatt.com
Website: www.johncatt.com

ISBN: 978 1 913622 96 1

Set and designed by John Catt Educational Limited

Reviews

This book illustrates research-informed practice at its best. Paul's rich teaching experience and his keen engagement with research has enabled him to get to the heart of classroom assessment. This book highlights how his dedication to Assessment for Learning has benefited learners and provides insights in understanding how AfL works.

Christine Harrison, Professor in Science Education, King's College London

Paul Spenceley, with a lifetime's experience of secondary science teaching, writes in great detail about everything he has learned originating from the King's College Assessment for Learning Project which led to the publication *Working Inside the Black Box*. This book is jam-packed with useful strategies which focus always on the learner and the learning, illustrated with nuanced discussion about the hows, whys, ifs and buts of the secondary classroom. Science teachers should read this book to transform their practice, not only for the power of formative assessment in furthering learning but also for ways in which summative assessment can be used effectively.

Shirley Clarke, international expert in formative assessment

Wherever you are in your teaching career, you will gain a lot from this book. It has made me reflect and challenge how I use assessment for learning in my lessons. It has simple, practical ideas on all aspects of teaching science. I have already tried some of these, with great success.

Jenny Walsh, chemistry teacher with 20 years of experience

Drawing on 20 years' thoughtful development of classroom assessment, Paul Spenceley shares and explains the fine details of practices that transform teaching and student learning. Every teacher (regardless of subject), teacher educator and school leader will find ideas to try immediately, and see how the interlinked elements build together into a powerful coherent approach to improving learning. The chapter showing how revising for, assessing, and reflecting on summative assessments can truly help students become better learners, as well as improving their test scores, is ground-breaking.

Sue Swaffield, Associate Professor, University of Cambridge

This was the first piece of writing on 'teaching and learning' that I have enjoyed reading; it was so easily accessible and what a game changer! I have already started using the measurable learning objectives and my students loved it! Especially at the end when they could actually see they had made progress (I had a lot of 'Wow, I'm actually good at science' comments).

Niamh Spinola, recently qualified teacher

Contents

Foreword

Dylan Wiliam, UCL Institute of Education

In his presidential address at the annual conference of the British Educational Research Association (BERA) in 1989, John Elliott (1990) argued that, to be relevant, educational researchers needed to forge stronger links with teachers, professional bodies, and policymakers. One concrete initiative emerging from this call was the establishment later that year of a number of Policy Task Groups focusing on assessment, curriculum, teacher education and local management of schools.

Over the next decade, the Assessment Policy Task Group (which became the Assessment Reform Group when BERA wound up the Policy Task Groups in 1996) produced a number of critiques of the education policy in England and Wales. However, as Richard Daugherty (2007) pointed out in his reflections on the work of the Group, these critiques had little impact because they were focused on changes that were already being implemented. Beginning in 1996, the group adopted a more strategic approach, and later that year, commissioned Paul Black and myself to produce a review of research on *classroom assessment*.

Our review (Black and Wiliam, 1998a) established a strong case that helping teachers develop their formative assessment practices would be likely to improve learning in classrooms. However, it was published in an academic journal to which most teachers would not have had access, it was long (almost 70 pages) and rather dense; one reviewer described it as a 'both elbows on the table read'.

To bring these findings to a wider audience, we wrote a short pamphlet, titled *Inside the Black Box* (Black and Wiliam, 1998b), in which we summarised the findings of our review, and drew out some implications for practitioners and policymakers. However, while the research showed the potential for formative assessment, it was not clear to us that it could be implemented in classrooms, especially those where teachers were under increasing pressure to improve test and examination results.

With help from Christine Harrison, then a lecturer in science education at King's, we therefore sought, and received, funding from the Nuffield Foundation for a project to work with science and mathematics teachers to see how the findings from our review might be used to improve classroom learning. We then approached assessment advisers in two local authorities – Medway and Oxfordshire – who helped us identify three schools in each authority that might be interested in working with us. We visited each of the six schools – which all agreed to participate – and the schools then nominated two mathematics teachers and two science teachers to participate in the project. Paul Spenceley was one of these.

Over the next year, we held a series of one-day meetings with Paul and the other 23 teachers with whom we shared our findings from the research and encouraged them to explore the implications for their own practice. At first, it seemed that the teachers thought we were operating a perverted model of discovery learning, where we knew what we wanted them to do but wanted them to discover it for themselves. After the third meeting, they realised that we really had no idea how these would play out in real classrooms, especially ones where teachers were under pressure to improve GCSE and A-level grades, and it really was up to them to figure out how to apply these research findings in their own classrooms. For our part, it became clear that applying research to practice in a field as complex as teaching is not just a process of dissemination, but rather that practitioners have to be involved in a process of knowledge creation, albeit of a distinct and local kind. The collaborative nature of the research was further emphasised by the fact that the participating teachers chose which formative assessment techniques they wanted to try out, which classes they would try these techniques with, what measures of achievement would be used to see if they were successful, and which other groups of students in the school would make suitable comparison groups. Paul and his colleague were especially keen to develop their questioning techniques.

The results of that project were published in a book for teachers (Black, Harrison, Lee, Marshall and Wiliam, 2003), a shorter summary titled *Working Inside the Black Box* (Black, Harrison, Lee, Marshall and Wiliam, 2002) and in a more technical journal article that showed a substantial impact on pupil achievement (Wiliam, Lee, Harrison and Black, 2004). However, the most enduring impact, for me, at least, was the way that teachers participating continued to work to improve their practice after the project had ended.

In the 20 years since that research project ended, Paul Spenceley – already a good teacher at the start of the project, and an outstanding one at the end – has continued to develop his practice of formative assessment, and to share his insights with other teachers, both at formal conferences, and also in more informal ways, such as supporting work of colleagues in his own and in other schools. This book describes, in an accessible and practical way, the development of his ideas about how to use assessment for learning in his own classroom, and how to support others in doing the same. Even though I have been researching and writing about formative assessment for over 25 years, I found much that was new, with great insights into the practicalities of formative assessment in real classrooms. I believe that every science teacher would gain enormously from reading this book and teachers of other subjects will also find much valuable insight into how to harness the power of assessment to improve, and not just measure, learning.

References

Black, P., Harrison, C., Lee, C., Marshall, B. and Wiliam, D. (2002) *Working inside the black box: Assessment for learning in the classroom.* London, UK: GL Assessment.

Black, P., Harrison, C., Lee, C., Marshall, B. and Wiliam, D. (2003) *Assessment for learning: Putting it into practice.* Buckingham, UK: Open University Press.

Black, P. and Wiliam, D. (1998a) 'Assessment and classroom learning.' *Assessment in Education: Principles, Policy and Practice*, 5(1): pp. 7-74.

Black, P. and Wiliam, D. (1998b) *Inside the black box: raising standards through classroom assessment.* London, UK: King's College London School of Education.

Daugherty, R. (2007) 'Mediating academic research: The Assessment Reform Group experience.' *Research Papers in Education*, 22(2): pp. 139-153. doi:10.1080/02671520701296072

Elliott, J. (1990) 'Educational research in crisis: Performance indicators and the decline in excellence.' *British Educational Research Journal*, 16(1): pp. 3-18. doi:10.1080/0141192900160101

Wiliam, D., Lee, C., Harrison, C. and Black, P. (2004) Teachers developing assessment for learning: impact on student achievement. *Assessment in Education: Principles Policy and Practice*, 11(1): pp. 49-65.

Who is Paul Spenceley?

Recently retired from teaching, I worked as a full-time, classroom science teacher throughout my career, always preferring the day-to-day challenges of teaching, rather than those of senior management.

I worked at a comprehensive school in Medway, Kent for 25 years, holding a range of posts including head of biology and head of science. This was very much the type of school that Tony Blair once described as a 'bog standard comprehensive' – an 11-18 co-educational school, with the full range of student abilities.

While teaching at this school between 1998 and 2001, I was involved in the King's College Formative Assessment Project led by Paul Black, Dylan Wiliam and Christine Harrison, that resulted in the publication of *Working Inside the Black Box* – still the definitive work on Assessment for Learning in secondary schools. This, in turn, led to Assessment for Learning being introduced as part of the National Teaching Strategy, and I was the sole teacher representative on the Department for Education committee that oversaw this. (Indeed, having an actual teacher involved in such a committee was apparently a rarity for the Department for Education!)

Following on from The King's Project, I was invited to talk on classroom-based Assessment for Learning in many schools, and at a variety of conferences in England and Scotland, which continued for the remainder of my teaching career, and beyond. In 2000 I was invited to Buckingham Palace for an evening to reward those who had 'made a significant contribution to education' as my local authority's sole secondary school teacher.

For the final nine years of my teaching career, I taught biology at a very high-achieving girls' grammar school, also in Medway. As the lead school in a highly successful trust, I had the opportunity to lead Assessment for Learning across several schools.

In January 2019 I was invited to join Paul Black and Christine Harrison to speak at the Association for Science Education's conference, to mark 20 years since the initial King's College Project. It was this milestone that made me start thinking of recording my experiences on using formative assessment in science lessons.

As a science teacher, I saw many government initiatives come and go during my career, mostly with little or no impact. However, the introduction of formative assessment techniques into my lessons, as a result of The King's College Project, not only greatly improved my teaching, but most importantly, greatly improved the learning by my students.

So, who is Paul Spenceley? A science teacher who passionately believes that other science teachers can improve their students' learning, not by working harder, but by simply doing all the things they already do, but slightly differently.

Introduction

Who is this book for?

As my teaching experience has almost all been in secondary schools, always as a science teacher, it seems only right that the ideas and examples that I have used throughout this book come from my own experiences. I think this is important for two reasons. Firstly, everything in this book is something that I have actually done with students of varying ages and abilities. There are no 'this sounds like a good idea in theory' bits; indeed, there is hardly any 'theory' at all. Secondly, science is often the area in secondary schools that finds it most difficult to adapt to new ideas and strategies. As I have often told teachers when delivering CPD sessions, if these ideas work in science, they will definitely work in other subjects too.

The book, therefore, is primarily aimed at science teachers. However, it should not be considered 'for their eyes only'. I have used science examples to illustrate the very best of classroom-based formative assessment techniques, but these ideas are not constrained to science lessons. Indeed, most of the techniques covered have been delivered in various whole-school CPD sessions, with great success. After all, rare is the teacher who does not have some form of discussion with students in their lessons, and surely non-existent is the teacher who does not have to plan lessons, or provide written feedback, or mark and return tests and exams to students. As these are key areas of this book, it follows that most classroom teachers will, I am sure, find something relevant.

For those teachers whose leadership roles leave them with little time for day-to-day classroom teaching, this book could provide a framework for an approach to teaching that has the potential to improve examination results, not just in science, but across the school. That may sound a big claim, but there is plenty of evidence to back it up.

This book is definitely *not* aimed at those looking for theoretical knowledge and deeper research on formative assessment or Assessment for Learning. There are already plenty of excellent books available that provide this. This is a 'read it then try it' book.

Nor is this book just for those starting out on a career in teaching, although it should prove useful for them. I was already a well-established and 'successful' science teacher before I even heard of formative assessment and Assessment for Learning, so even if you have 'seen it all before', I would like to suggest that there will be something in this book that makes you stop and think about your day-to-day work in the classroom. After all, the key point of this book is that everything included has helped students to improve their learning and, as a result, their achievements. So, if that is your aim too, then this book is for you.

Finally, and most importantly, nothing in this book should involve teachers doing more work – they already do more than enough. So, this book is definitely *not* about adding to the burden of teaching. If, however, you want to improve your students learning – and results – without doing any more work, this book is aimed at you.

Terminology problems

Having said that this is not a book about education theory, I do, however, feel that it is essential to clarify the use of some of the terminology used throughout. This is important, as some of the key terminology has been used in different ways, by different educationalists, and unfortunately, the same phrases can often mean different things to different people. As such, I want to clarify my use of three vital phrases.

When I was first introduced to the ideas and methods described in this book, in order to clarify terminology, Paul Black provided the following definitions:

Summative assessment – *assessment that is used to provide evidence of achievement by students*. In science, these are often tests or exams, although they could be write-ups of practicals, etc.

Formative assessment – *assessment that is used to provide evidence for improvement in learning by students*. These are the techniques and methods that I will mainly focus on in this book.

However, such was the importance of the findings of The King's College Project, and their summation in *Working Inside the Black Box*, that the Department for Education introduced another term, **Assessment for Learning**, which they used as a synonym for the formative assessment ideas and techniques. Thus, the term **AfL** became used commonly in schools to represent all forms of formative assessment, whereas Paul Black and Dylan Wiliam would argue that formative assessment is actually a subset of AfL.

At this point, you might think: (a) who cares? and (b) is this really important? Well, I just want to make it clear that in this book I will sometimes use the phrase Assessment for Learning when I am describing formative assessment methods and techniques. It's simply because my experience shows me that the majority of teachers and senior leaders in schools have been used to using this phrase for almost 20 years now.

What is classroom-based Assessment for Learning?

This book focuses completely on classroom-based Assessment for Learning (as summarised by The Assessment Reform Group) which I will refer to simply as AfL from now on. But what actually is classroom-based AfL?

I would be considerably richer in my retirement years if I had been given £10 each time a teacher or member of the senior management at a school had told me that they had 'done' AfL, as if it were yet another thing to be ticked off on the long list of ideas and strategies that seem to be forever 'coming down from above', before the 'next thing' has to be moved on to.

In the same way I could have added to my retirement fund if I had received £10 each time an exasperated teacher had said words such as, 'I can't do any more than I already am' or 'There isn't the time', suggesting that AfL was yet another burden to be added to their already overloaded teaching load.

Another boost to my retirement lifestyle would have come from being given £10 each time a science teacher had said to me, 'But science is different from other subjects' or suggested that because of the amount of content, 'there isn't time in science'. The 'teach a topic, test, moan about results, move on' hamster wheel of science teaching is something very difficult for some staff to see beyond. I know this only too well, as I spent many years of my career on that same hamster wheel.

So, let me start with my views on what classroom-based AfL is *not*. AfL is not something that is 'added' to lessons in the way that, for example, a vocabulary test might be added to help to improve subject-specific literacy. Nor is AfL something that is 'done' and then moved on from. AfL is also not something that needs a spreadsheet to prove that it is being done. Finally, AfL is not about target grades, 'flight pathways', hierarchical learning objectives, or any of the other multitude of ways schools seem to have evolved for tracking or pigeon-holing students and their progress.

To me, AfL is a very simple thing to define: it is a *way of teaching*, nothing more or less.

From my earliest involvement on The King's College Project, formative assessment techniques permeated everything I did as a teacher, within the classroom and as a leader within a department. I hope that this book will help to bring this idea across, although this approach to AfL does cause me its own problems. For logistical reasons, the book is divided into chapters, focused on different aspects of teaching. However, by the very nature of AfL as 'all-encompassing', as I see it, I will apologise now for the fact that many ideas will occur in more than one place within the book. This is not just me simply trying to improve the word count, but my attempt to show how the various chapters and ideas are not a 'box of chocolates' from which the best can be selected, but together form a different way of approaching the teaching of science. One that, hopefully, will allow some more science teachers off the hamster wheel, and in turn improve the learning and achievement of more students, in what many find a 'difficult' subject.

Chapter 1
Planning for learning

Introduction – teaching and learning

I can still remember (just about) when I first started teaching, when I was busy planning lessons that I thought would last me a lifetime – after all, surely teaching eleven-year-olds about cells was always going to be the same, wasn't it? Later in my career, when computers and presentations took over, I still remember thinking that now I would be able to save all my lesson plans and presentations, and that they would never have to be done again. So, if you are reading this, having just started out on a career as a science teacher, can I firstly get the bad news out of the way. Planning lessons is something that teachers do throughout their careers. No matter how many times you might have previously taught a topic, or however many presentations you may have saved, lessons will always need planning. There will never be a time when all your lesson planning is 'done'. I'm sorry if that comes as a shock to you, but it's a fact. Lessons need planning, and with AfL being a way of teaching, for me, then it makes sense that when starting out on planning, AfL and formative assessment techniques need to be involved in that process.

Before I get started, can I point out that one of the biggest problems that I see with teachers is that they always want to concentrate on teaching! I think this is really annoying, because if instead of being called 'teachers' we had a different title – say 'facilitators of learning' – then maybe we would all take a different approach. But let's be honest: 'facilitator of learning' sounds like some sort of weird 'politically correct' language, not from the real world. So, we are teachers, but that does *not* mean we have to plan what we are going to teach. We should be planning what students are going to learn. I can hear now, sighs and groans, as readers start to think this is going to be one of those exercises where we just call something by a new name, when it's all the same really. Trust me, it is *not* the same. I'm reminded of a story, where a young girl tells her friend that she has taught her hamster to dance. Her friend is very excited, as said hamster is removed from its cage and placed on a table. The hamster does nothing more than hamsters usually do. The friend, predictably, is not impressed. 'I thought you said you had taught your hamster to dance,' she says. 'I did,' the girl replies. 'I didn't say the hamster had learned it.' And herein lies the final way, in which my retirement fund could have been boosted. If only I had even £5 for each time I heard a colleague say to a class, 'But I taught them that last lesson/week/year.' Admit it, you can remember using just such a phrase yourself. Well, if nothing else, planning for learning, if done properly, should mean never having to say those words again.

1:1 Planning individual lessons – learning objectives

I am going to start by assuming that readers know the basics of lesson planning and the terminology involved.

Having been provided with some exam specification statements, or internally derived statements, on what it is required of the students in a lesson, the starting point of planning for learning should be the learning objectives. Here, science teachers (although they are not alone I may add) often seem to have problems. The first problem seems to have been an acceptance over the years since learning objectives first became the norm, to think that adding the phrase 'to be able to' at the start of a statement will instantly transform it into a learning objective. The second problem with learning objectives is when many schools insist on staff using hierarchical learning objectives of some sort. Here, teachers seem to spend most of their time and energy on trying to fit their 'all', 'most' or 'some' ideas, or Bloom's taxonomy phrases (see page 56), into their statements. The final, and biggest, problem with learning objectives, is that they tend to be about **teaching**, and to be for the *teacher*, rather than **learning**, and for the *students*.

The end result of all of this is that I have seen, on sadly too many occasions, learning objectives such as: 'To be able to describe photosynthesis' or 'To be able to describe and explain how heat is transferred.'

So, what is wrong with these as learning objectives? Well, as overall *aims* of a lesson for the teachers use, these would be fine, but as learning objectives to help students to improve *their learning*, they are of little use.

Let's look at the first of these: 'To be able to describe photosynthesis.' At first glance, this looks perfectly clear, and if you asked students what they were going to learn during the lesson, they would happily repeat that they were 'learning how to describe photosynthesis'. But think about this statement a bit more. This same learning objective could be used at key stage 3, GCSE or A-level. Clearly it would not mean the same thing at each of these stages, but herein lies one of the big problems with learning objectives. Often only the teacher has a really clear idea what is actually required for the learning objective to be met. Now this is fine IF the teacher constantly explains the requirements for success to the students throughout the lesson, but in practice this rarely happens. Instead, usually the learning objective remains the teacher's property, and only he/she really knows what actually needs to be *learned* by the students.

The second learning objective also seems clear enough at first glance, and although it is subdivided into two parts, these are clear. However, with all 'higher level' learning objectives, such as 'to explain', or 'to analyse', 'to evaluate', etc., the same problem occurs, with the teacher having a clear idea of what is required to meet the objective, but the students not really knowing *exactly* what they need to do in order to demonstrate learning. Think of this learning objective from the students' viewpoint: how many descriptions or explanations are needed? Does a simple explanation suffice? Or is a more complex explanation required?

The key point about a learning objective should be that from reading it, the students should be aware of *exactly* what they need to do during the lesson in order to be *successful learners*. Thought of in this way, a learning objective becomes much more of a success criterion, which in many cases students are used to using from primary schools. To illustrate the importance of proper learning objectives, I will use an anecdote, before going on to illustrate how subtly different wording can totally alter the usefulness, to students, of a learning objective. This anecdote is a little long, but it will hopefully make its point clearly by the end.

A time when polar bears were not white...

Soon after starting my involvement with The King's College Project, focusing on formative assessment in science, I was working with a very low-achieving Year 11 group on adaptations of animals to cold climates. This is traditionally done by using the polar bear as an example. As the students had extremely low literacy skills, they typed answers to pre-prepared questions and tasks on a computer. One of the questions asked, 'What advantage is it for a polar bear to be the colour it is?' Timmy, one of the students, needed the question read and explained to him, so I explained that the question wanted to know why polar bears were the colour they were. Timmy said he did not know what colour polar bears were. So, I referred him back to the image of a polar bear at the start of the work, which showed a slightly creamy-coloured polar bear, in the snow. When I checked on Timmy later, he had typed, 'Polar bears are ylw (sic. yellow) but I still don't know why they are ylw.' Can you imagine an Ofsted inspector coming into my lesson at that point? (First mention of the dreaded O word!) If they had looked at Timmy's work, it would look like he had been poorly taught, and was definitely not learning very much.

Later in the lesson, there was a plenary, which consisted of the students (a small group) sitting round a large table and sharing their ideas about their learning. When I asked Timmy how his learning had gone, he said that he was 'over halfway through the learning objectives'. When I asked him to justify this, Timmy explained that the first learning objective had asked for at least three adaptations of polar bears to cold weather to be stated, and that he knew two: thick fur and small ears. He then said that the second learning objective had asked for at least three adaptations of polar bears to cold climates to be explained.

Timmy then explained why the bears had thick fur and small ears. He said that because he could not do three examples for each, he was not prepared to fully award himself either of the learning objectives – mainly because he still did not know why polar bears were yellow. Think again, if an Ofsted inspector had heard Timmy at this point of the lesson, being able to accurately evaluate the level of his own learning. I am certain the inspector would have been extremely impressed.

One of the other students in the group then raised hibernation as an adaptation. After some discussion on whether or not adaptations had to be an actual physical part of the polar bear, hibernation was finally accepted by the students. At this point Timmy declared that he felt that he had now achieved both learning objectives, as he now knew three adaptations, and could explain all three – promptly offering his correct explanation of hibernation.

The point that I hope that you can see from this – totally true – anecdote, is that even the least academically able students are able to understand what *learning* actually is, and to what extent they have learned during a lesson, providing that they are given learning objectives that contain clear *success criteria*.

If Timmy had faced the much more common, 'To be able to describe and explain the adaptations of animals to cold climates,' he would not only have been unable to articulate the degree of his learning, but he would undoubtedly not have even known what level of learning was required from him. Instead, Timmy had been given the following two learning objectives:

'To be able to state at least three adaptations that polar bears have to help them to survive in cold climates'

and

'To be able to explain how at least three adaptations help polar bears to survive in cold climates.'

I will restate that with the original 'vague' learning objective, IF the teacher had constantly mentioned the success criteria during the lesson, the same outcome would have occurred, but this is often very difficult to do. It is far easier to have learning objectives that actually clarify success criteria as much as possible for the *students* to be able to see, and know for themselves, exactly what learning is required of them.

By the way, just to put your minds at rest, Timmy later discovered during the plenary discussion that polar bears were in fact white, and why they were.

Using clear success criteria in learning objectives

So, let's look again one of the earlier unclear examples of a learning objective: 'To be able to describe what happens during photosynthesis.'

This could have instead been broken up, and written instead as:

'To be able to state the two reactants and two products of photosynthesis'

and

'To be able to describe at least one thing that happens to each of the products of photosynthesis.'

With these, it would be much clearer for the *students* to know what they actually needed to do in order to succeed in their learning. Looking at these reworded learning objectives, it is also much clearer that they are aimed at KS3, and clearly not A-level.

Using numbers of examples required for descriptions or explanations is an easy way to make a learning objective clearer to students. As with Timmy, this also allows students to 'measure' the success of their learning. Adding 'at least' before the number, means that any student who is slightly quicker at doing a particular task, can't just say, 'I'm finished,' as soon as they get to the minimum number, allowing for a very basic level of differentiation.

With explanations, it is often helpful to ask for students to give a specific number of different reasons for something happening, e.g.:

'To be able to give at least two simple reasons why a radiator works better if nearer the floor than the ceiling.'

This is so much more informative for the students than simply asking them to 'explain why radiators are usually nearer the floor'.

Similarly, when being asked to evaluate, the learning objective should make it clear how many 'positive' and 'negative' points are needed about something, and also whether or not the students need to then draw their own conclusion, and if they need to say why they have made the choice, e.g. 'To be able to provide at least four pieces of evidence to support the argument *for* global warming, and at least four pieces of evidence which *oppose* the argument for global warming' followed by 'To be able to use your evidence to provide a conclusion on the likelihood that global warming is a man-made phenomenon.'

Notice how in these examples, not only is the learning task clearer to the students, but the *level* of learning required is also more apparent – no more confusion over which key stage a learning objective is for.

Numbers are not the only way of making learning objectives clearer for students, and they may not always work. However, hopefully, these examples have made you realise the difference between basic learning objectives – literally what you hope the students will learn – and *success criteria*, which reflect the level of performance in a learning task. During planning, if you focus on exactly what successful learning will *look like*, and you articulate this to the students, then already you have started **planning for learning**, rather than planning for teaching.

Learning objectives like this will inevitably be longer than the more straightforward 'aims' which are so often used, but they will allow students to play a full, and active, part in *their own learning* during the lesson, and that is step one in using AfL as a *different way of teaching*.

So, as mentioned in the introduction, this technique does *not* involve more work. You will still be planning learning objectives for lessons; they will just be worded differently. Soon, it will become second nature to do them like this.

I will finish this section with a quote from an experienced head of maths at the very successful girls' grammar school where I taught. Following a CPD session on planning for learning, she came and said to me a couple of weeks later, 'I have always got 2/1 (good, almost outstanding) for my lesson observations, although my lessons have always gone all to plan, and I have felt the students have all learned everything. After your CPD session, I tried rewording my learning objectives, to make them clearer to the students. During my next observation I got a 1 (outstanding). The observer said it was great to see students discussing their own learning, against clearly measurable objectives. I can't believe the difference it has made. Thank you.'

1:2 Planning individual lessons – plenaries

Having mastered the art of writing useful learning objectives for your lesson, the temptation by most teachers is to then plan what they are going to *teach*, to enable the students to be able to learn what is required of them. This is then usually followed by planning one or more plenaries, which will check the teaching that has been done. Unfortunately, this is still planning for teaching, *not* for learning. Inevitably if this is done – if time is short for whatever reason – at the end of the lesson, the teacher rushes to complete the teaching or tasks, and either rushes, or scraps the plenary entirely. Admit it, you can remember a time when you did not 'have time' for a plenary. That happened because you planned for *teaching, not learning*.

Having planned the learning objectives with a clear idea of what the *success criteria* should be, if the lesson emphasis is on learning, then the next stage should obviously be to plan the plenary/plenaries, which will be used to measure the success of the students' learning. At this point you may, again, be tempted to think that this is just a matter of semantics, and that the order of the planning is irrelevant. It is not. After the learning objectives, the plenary (let's assume that whenever I use the singular, there may be more than one) is the next most important part of the lesson, and should be given that priority in your mind. If you plan it last, as almost an afterthought, you are subconsciously downgrading the importance of the plenary in your own mind, even if you do not mean to do so.

Let's think for a moment about the lesson about the polar bears (page 20). If there had not been a properly planned plenary, or perhaps time had run out and the plenary had been sacrificed, Timmy would have left the lesson thinking polar bears were yellow, but been unsure why. More importantly, he would have been unsure if he had succeeded in learning during that lesson, having been aware that prior to the plenary he had not met either of the learning objectives. The time to share ideas, during the plenary, was itself a vital part of the learning.

Knowing the success criteria for the lesson usually makes it easier to decide which type of plenary would be most useful. I will only look at a few examples here, as there are many excellent ideas of plenaries available on the internet. What is most important is that the type of plenary should clearly allow the *students* to be able to *measure* their success against the learning objectives. There is little point in having really clear success criteria about what needs to be learned, then using a past exam question as the plenary that covers only one small part of one of the learning objectives. That is not to say that a past exam question is not a good plenary, but it must suit the success criteria you are looking to evaluate. There are, for example, good exam questions that could have been used with Timmy's group, asking for adaptations to be labelled on a drawing of a polar bear, and to explain these adaptations in writing. The key point here is not just using a plenary idea because it looks 'different', or because you have not used the particular idea for a while, but to plan which type of plenary best allows the students to *see their own learning*. Hopefully you will realise as you read on that different plenary ideas will better suit different learning objectives, and success criteria, and that a combination of plenary ideas may be needed to fully measure students' learning.

All of the following plenary ideas have been successfully used across the whole range of ages and spectrum of abilities during science lessons, with great success.

Plenary ideas

Discussions as plenaries are an excellent idea, but in practice these can be difficult to use. As a result, these will be looked at in detail in chapter 2. At this point, however, it is just necessary to say that the discussions should clearly give the students the opportunity to evaluate their learning against the success criteria, in the same way the anecdote about Timmy (page 20) did earlier. This is far from easy to do, which is why the whole of chapter 2 is devoted to discussions.

Past exam questions as plenaries are often useful, along with exam board specifications, at helping to decide on the wording of the success criteria in the learning objectives. For example, with the adaptations of animals to cold climates, it would be pointless looking at many different animals during the lesson, if all the past exam questions focus on polar bears. Similarly, it would be pointless insisting on seven or eight adaptations if past questions never ask for more than two. By using the specification statements and past exam questions, measuring of learning can often be clearly done. It may be necessary to use a couple of different exam questions to check the learning of all the lesson's learning objectives. Or an exam question may be used to check learning of one learning objective, with a different plenary idea used to check another learning objective.

Multiple-choice questions make great plenaries. However, too often these allow students to 'guess' and do not make it clear to the students what *successful learning* actually is. There are two ways to solve this. Firstly, if using single correct answer multiple-choice questions, then a clear number of correct answers required should be stated before starting them, as a measure of success, e.g. 'In order to be able to say that you have fully completed the first learning objective, you should be able to get at least seven out of these 10 questions right.'

The second way of using multiple-choice questions as plenaries is to have more than one, or perhaps even none, of the answers correct, so that the students are no longer able to just guess, and need to make better use of their learning. As before, the students will need to be told what success will look like in terms of marks. Having more than one correct answer, or perhaps no correct answers at all, in a multiple-choice question, does much more than just stop students from guessing. It also forces them to read, and consider, all of the answers very carefully, rather than focusing on the one answer that they feel 'looks right'. Having several correct answers can also mean that less questions need to be completed in order to measure the success of a particular learning objective. The other benefit of this technique is that it is a very simple method of differentiation.

3-2-1 plenaries can be adapted in all sorts of ways, but again can be tailored to specific success criteria. You could, for example, easily use this idea when the learning objective asks for students to 'evaluate' something, as follows:

3 – Facts/reasons why X could/did (not) happen.

2 – Facts/reasons why X could/did (not) happen.

1 – Fact/reason that made you decide on your overall conclusion.

Another way in which 3-2-1 plenaries can be used is to check general learning, maybe part way through, or at the end, of a lesson. For example:

3 – New facts/explanations you have learned so far about...

2 – Facts/explanations you already knew, but have added more to your learning about...

1 – Fact/explanation that you want to know more about as the lesson goes on/would like more time to find out about/would like help to understand.

The final one of these three is particularly powerful as a way of gauging where students feel insecure, and because it follows on from the previous two statements where they were probably more secure, you will usually find that students get 'on a roll' with their 3-2-1, and tend to be much more productive here, than if a statement simply asking for things they were 'unsure of' were used alone.

An alternative method of using this type of plenary that links to self-assessment (see chapter 4) might be as follows, where students are asked to use different colours to highlight the following things in their work:

3 – Pieces of evidence that prove that you have achieved learning objective one.

2 – Most important pieces of information you will need in the future to answer an exam question on learning objective 2.

1 – Piece of evidence that you would like to know more about/need help with.

The key idea with all 3-2-1 plenaries is that the plenary is itself hierarchical in terms of the level of thinking required by students to complete the three tasks, with the **3** always being an easier task to complete than the **1**, and with the third statement often, but not always, being the most useful to the teacher.

Spot the misatke plenaries (did you see what I did there?) are a good way of checking learning of facts, descriptions or explanations. A list of statements is given to the students based on information that should have been learned if the learning objectives have been properly mastered. Students then have to find how many of these statements are incorrect. For example, students may be given five facts about the periodic table and be asked to state how many (if any) are false. It is always best if on occasion none of the statements are incorrect, so that students do not resort to simply 'guessing'.

This type of plenary can be varied, or differentiated, so that maybe only part of a statement is incorrect at higher levels. 'Spot the mistake' plenaries are particularly useful for checking on common errors or misconceptions. For example, many students think that light rays travel from their eyes towards objects, which they see. Similarly, many students think the arrows in food chains show what animals eat, rather than the energy flow. Both of these, and many other misconceptions, can be fairly easily and quickly tested using 'spot the mistake' plenaries.

To avoid students simply guessing, as well as occasionally having no incorrect statements, it is a good idea to state how many errors students are allowed to make, e.g. 'There are seven statements here on today's work, and I will expect you to say correctly if at least five of them are right or wrong, to truly demonstrate you have achieved today's learning objectives.'

'Spot the mistake' plenaries can easily be extended by asking students to correct the information, or to explain why it is wrong, rather than simply stating that it is. This could easily turn into part or all of a home learning task, or even the starter of the following lesson, e.g. 'Here are the statements you looked at in the plenary last lesson. Can you remember how many were incorrect? For each incorrect one, write a short explanation of why it is wrong, for today's starter.'

Explaining learning objective plenaries can be done in small groups, or with individuals chosen at random to speak to the whole class. The idea is that the individual chosen is asked to 'describe/explain/evaluate' a particular learning objective, e.g. 'Can you please explain to your group how one of the three methods for insulating a house against heat loss works.' This works well with groups if there are the same number of students in a group as the number of learning objectives. So, for example, each person in a group of three, could be asked to explain one of the three methods of heat loss. This is a good plenary for checking progress part way through a lesson, although obviously it would work equally as well at the end of the lesson.

This type of plenary can also be linked to self-assessment, which will be covered later in chapter 4 (see page 111). As with all discussion work, the important part of this plenary is that the teacher not only listens to the various responses provided by individual students, but also considers the response of the other students in the group to what they are hearing. For example, if one person in a group of three gives an excellent explanation of radiation when describing heat loss, but the other two students in the group seem totally perplexed by the explanation, this is vital information for the teacher on the overall level of learning within the class – or of particular individuals. The key point with these 'explaining learning objective' plenaries is that the response of *all* students, not only those speaking at any one time, is important.

A slight variation may be to ask the students to explain where the evidence is in their work that would justify a particular learning objective, and why they think this. So a student, instead of describing convection, may be asked to find the *evidence* that shows they understand convection, and why they think the evidence is good enough to prove their learning.

Traffic light key words or phrases plenaries are another simple method of discovering where students have, or lack, confidence in their learning. At the end of the lesson the teacher would provide the students with a number of facts, explanations, etc. These could be on an interactive whiteboard or on cut out pieces of paper. The students would then be asked individually to group the various statements as follows:

Green – Facts/explanations that I was already pretty sure of before today's lesson.

Amber – Facts/explanations that I have learned and understood during today's lesson.

Red – Facts/explanations that I am not fully confident with still.

There will be more on the idea of students traffic lighting to show confidence in chapter 5, however, at this stage it is worth noting that there is clear evidence to show that low-achieving students do tend to overstate their confidence, which needs to be borne in mind. It would not take a great deal of prior planning to use the 'red' section as targeted home learning, with textbooks or resources available for individuals. The benefit here, of course, is that the students have identified the need for the 'extra' learning that they need to do, rather than seeing their home learning task as simply a form of punishment.

Guessing the learning objectives plenaries are good fun to do occasionally with groups who are used to *clearly defined success criteria* in their learning objectives. In this case, the students would be told that they were not being given learning objectives at the start of the lesson, but that they would be expected to generate their own at the end of the lesson – they would need to be told how many they would need to generate. The students would need to be reminded during the lesson to think about what the learning objectives might be, while they are working on their lesson tasks. At the end of the lesson, random students could be chosen to suggest wording for learning objectives. Perhaps, for example, you could select three different possible ways of wording the first learning objective, and then either select another student to decide, or have a class vote on the 'best' one.

An adaptation to a 'guessing the learning objectives' plenary might be to divide the lesson into clear sections, each with a learning objective, and to ask different groups of students to identify the learning objective for each section of the lesson, e.g. 'During this first section of the lesson, I would like the first 10 students on the register to think about what the learning objective might be.' In this way, it is also possible to differentiate, so that lower attaining students, within the group, are given easier learning objectives to 'guess'.

There are, as I said earlier, many, many more examples of plenaries available. However, there are some very important things to consider with any plenary when planning lessons for learning. Firstly, the plenary must *always* be specifically tailored to allow the success criteria in the learning objectives to be *measured*. Secondly, the plenary should clearly and plainly enable the *students* to measure *for themselves* the level of progress they have made. Finally, *enough time* must be planned into the lesson to ensure that these two points are met. If these three key things are remembered, then I am certain that just about any plenary could easily be used, or adapted, to provide useful information on progress in learning.

1:3 Planning individual lessons – the starter

Having decided on the learning objectives with success criteria to make learning clear, and your plenary to measure the success of the learning, *only now* should you move on to the next step and plan the starter.

For many teachers, the starter is seen entirely as an activity to gain the attention of and stimulate the students. Although both of these are important, if a lesson is planned for *learning*, then it follows that at the start of the lesson the *prior level of learning* needs to be ascertained. Too often, this aspect of a starter is neglected, with many teachers working on the assumption that if something had been *taught* previously, then it has, therefore, been *learned* previously. In this way, many lessons fall into the trap of making assumptions on the progress that students will make. This is undoubtedly a major cause of unsatisfactory progress being made by the majority of students in some science lessons.

It is relatively easy to plan starter activities that establish the previous level of learning, but still involve a fun and engaging task for the students to do. What is important is, as with plenaries, the starter needs to be focused on measuring the previous learning, rather than assuming it has taken place. For this reason, starters can often be versions of plenaries, but planned to include a bit more 'instant impact'.

As with plenaries, there are many examples of starters online but, hopefully, those listed below will show how basic starter ideas can be adapted, if necessary, to include a measure of prior learning. It is often possible to use ideas as either plenaries or starters, as obviously both should be designed to check learning. So, for example, there is no reason why an adapted version of a 'spot the mistakes' plenary could not be used as a starter, as described in the section on plenaries above.

One of the key aspects of using a starter to measure prior learning, should be to identify areas of concern, or misconceptions, in that learning. This will mean that in many cases, it will be what students do *not* say or do *not* include in their starter activity that the teacher should often be most interested in.

Starter ideas

Discussion starters are excellent ways of checking prior learning, if they are handled properly. They are also the 'go to' starter for many science lessons, although far too often without the effectiveness that they could easily have. As mentioned earlier, this topic will be covered fully in chapter 2, but at this point it is worth noting that to provide worthwhile information on actual learning, discussions need to be very carefully planned. At this stage, I would *not* suggest using a discussion as a starter (or as a plenary) until you have read chapter 2.

Crossword starters are a very good way to check that students have recalled prior vocabulary that will be needed for the upcoming lesson. One way of doing these is to get students to build on a key word or short phrase, as seen in the example below. Here the single word *photosynthesis* was provided by the teacher, and students were asked to add any other relevant vocabulary from their former learning on to this word. Students can be told to aim for a particular number of words, which could be differentiated with 'At least…', or given an absolute minimum number of additional words that they must add to the crossword. This is a quick and easy method to see if any previously taught key words have not actually been learned. A quick discussion could, if necessary, be used to check understanding of the terms, and give some indication of prior *learning*, rather than prior *teaching*.

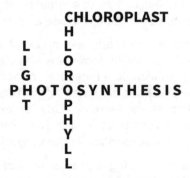

An alternative version of this starter would see different students, or groups of students, being given different starter words or phrases and then feeding back their answers to the whole class. This would work particularly well if the starter was for the first lesson of a topic, which was building on earlier learning. So, for example, one group may be given *conductors*, and another *insulators*, as their starter words. Or different groups of students could be given *group 1 metals*, *group 2 metals*, *halogens*, *transition metals* and *inert gases* to check prior learning on the periodic table. Each group could then be asked to provide feedback to the class.

3-2-1 starters can be a quick way of checking prior knowledge and can be adapted in many ways, as with 3-2-1 plenaries. For example, students who had recently been taught basic work on series and parallel circuits, and who were due to move on to measure current and voltage in the two types of circuit, might be asked to provide:

3 – Differences between series and parallel circuits.

2 – Advantages for using parallel circuits to light a house.

1 – Thing that they think other people might have forgotten or that they think some people might not have fully understood about series and parallel circuits.

A quick check of these, especially the final one, will give useful information about prior learning, rather than teaching. Asking students to say one thing that *other* students might have forgotten, or might not have fully understood, will usually highlight areas of concern for the students themselves, without the students actually having to admit to having the problem.

An alternative way of using a 3-2-1 starter in the same circumstances might be as follows:

3 – Facts about series and parallel circuits that you must know to answer exam questions.

2 – Explanations about series and parallel circuits that you would need to answer exam questions.

1 – Thing that might make exam questions on series and parallel circuits difficult.

These two versions of the same basic 3-2-1 starter will hopefully make it clear how flexible this is as an idea, and as with crossword starters there is no reason why different students, or groups of students, could not be given different starters, which they could then feed back to the rest of the class. This would again be particularly useful, for example, as a starter for a major topic, which is developing earlier learning.

Shared diagram starters are a fun way to check on previous learning. This works best with complex diagrams, such as a typical cell, the structure of the eye, an outline of the periodic table, an outline of the electromagnetic spectrum, etc. The key point is that the diagram should contain a lot of previously taught information. Students usually work in pairs, using a single sheet of A3 paper, and will be given the task of drawing and annotating, let's say, a typical plant cell. After about a minute, or whenever most pairs have made a start on the outline, and added perhaps one structure, the students are asked to stop. They are then asked to leave their work, move to another table, and continue to work on the diagram they find there. This keeps happening, every minute, with students moving on to ever more completed diagrams. They will need to be reminded to check for any errors, and alter these, as well as adding any of their own information. Ideally this would continue until the students have moved through all the other diagrams, and find themselves back at their own one, which should now be complete. This is a great fun way of checking which students have remembered which parts of their former learning, as well as highlighting any clear misunderstandings held by individuals, or the whole class. I have varied this idea to use 'plant cell' on one side of the paper and 'animal cell' on the other, with students turning the paper over halfway through their time slot. This has worked very well at both GCSE and A-level. Watching and listening to individuals as they complete the task is always very informative. Differentiation of this starter can be quite simple, for example, by asking for more or less detail in annotations, or simply for labels rather than annotations, if necessary.

Video expert starters are a great way of finding out any areas of prior knowledge and understanding that students lack confidence with. This works by asking the students to imagine that they are going to make a video about a particular topic that they have been taught before, which would be useful for today's lesson. They are asked to say which part of their previous teaching they would invite 'an expert' to explain on the video, and why they think that it would be useful to have an expert for this section. Clearly, this starter immediately forces the students to think about areas of concern in their prior learning.

An important point here is that video expert starters allow students to identify areas of concern that they may have in their learning, without them having to directly show their own weaknesses to others. For example, when doing this with one group with the topic on heat exchange, one girl said she would invite an expert to explain 'convection, because conduction and radiation are quite straightforward, but people get muddled with convection, density, and all that stuff.' It would be very unlikely, if the girl had been asked directly, that she would have so readily owned up to misunderstanding convection, and even less likely that she would have highlighted her lack of clarity about the role of density. By being able to say, 'People get muddled by...' this made the admission less personal, but provided me, as the teacher, with vital information on her learning.

On occasion I have even combined the video expert and 3-2-1 starter ideas. For example, the students were told that they were going to direct a video on a prior topic, and that they had to decide:

3 – Pieces of information your video will contain to describe/explain the topic.

2 – Images/diagrams your video will contain to describe/explain the topic.

1 – Piece of information you will invite an expert to describe/ explain about the topic.

This combined starter is particularly useful for a revision lesson on a sizeable topic of previous work. In fact, I have even developed this to become the focus for part of, or all of, a revision lesson, where students went on to produce a script/storyboard for their video.

Fishtail diagram starters are a good way of checking prior learning of large topics, such as energy, forces, the periodic table, cells, etc. These work particularly well at the start of a new topic that builds on previous learning. The fishtails are pre-printed (A3 paper works best) with the topic stated in the fish head (see example below). Students, perhaps working in pairs, are then given one minute to discuss what they remember about the topic with a partner, then one minute to write any key information onto the fishbones. The students then leave their work and move to another table. Here, they are given one minute to read what has already been written on the fishbones, and then a minute to add to any further information written by other students on the bones. (They may be allowed to correct the information already written.) In this way, as students continue to move around the room, more time will be needed for reading, and it will gradually be harder for students to recall additional information, as previous students are likely to have already done so. By carefully observing the progress of the information recorded, and individual students, it is fairly easy for the teacher to identify areas of weakness in prior learning of the group as a whole, or of particular students.

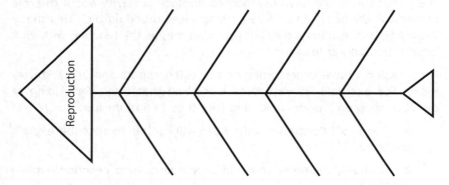

A quicker version of fishtail diagram starters could be done using the same idea and randomly selected individuals on an interactive whiteboard. I have even observed a teacher doing just this, who simply wrote 'last lessons work' in the fish head.

As always, it was what students forgot, or muddled, that was probably of most importance to the teacher.

I went shopping starters use the idea of the party game, where students have to add to a growing list of learned information. This not only allows prior learning to be judged, but also ensures students have to be focused on what other students are saying, which is always a bonus! (It will often come as a surprise how easily some students, who never seem to be able to listen to others, find this starter easy to do, because it is a 'game' rather than 'work'!) Instead of shopping, the starter sentence would be something like, 'When we did the work on … I learned …' This sentence could be specifically tailored to various levels of learning, such as 'I can describe...' or 'I can explain...' As with most starters that assess prior learning, it is often what students do *not* say, as much – if not more – than what they do, which will provide the most insight for the teacher. As with the fishtail diagrams, this works best with larger topics, for example, 'When we did the work on chemical reactions I learned...' Teachers always seem surprised by how many things students remember during this starter, but should also be aware, as always, of the things missing from the students' lists.

Adding time starters are another way of identifying areas of concern in the prior learning of students. Similar to the video expert idea above, this gives students the opportunity to highlight areas where they lack clarity or understanding. The students need to be made aware that the extra time added to their previous work would need to be used to enhance their learning, not to watch a video, etc. For example, 'If you could have had one more lesson on the topic of ... what would you like to have explained again?' Or, perhaps more precisely, 'If you could have had an extra 15 minutes on last lesson's work, what would have helped you to better be able to describe/explain ...?' (The rest of this sentence should directly reflect a learning objective from the previous lesson, using identical wording.)

This starter can be expanded by asking other students to suggest some solutions. For example, if a student says that they would like more time spent on balancing chemical equations because they still struggle with them, the teacher could ask other students for one or two tips on how to do this. This will not only help the individual, but also highlight how deep the problem of balancing chemical equations might be within the particular groups of students.

Taking turns with a partner starters are a good way of being able to identify exactly which individuals have, or have not, got confidence in particular areas of their prior learning of a topic. Students are simply asked to take it in turns to tell their partner anything at all they can remember learning about the required topic. Students continue to take turns until one of them is unable to continue. This could be based on a general topic or a particular learning objective. For example, 'Last lesson you learned about electron shells in atoms. Take it in turns with your partner to state any facts you can remember about electron shells.'

Various rules can be set, such as: how long a student is allowed to pause for while thinking before they are 'out', whether key words/phrases have to be defined, what happens if the information is incorrect, etc. These rules can obviously be used to differentiate the same starter for higher or lower attainers in the group.

'Taking turns with a partner' starters often give students more confidence, than when being asked to speak to the whole class. Teachers often note that during these starters one student will sometimes help, or encourage, the other with small hints, etc. What is particularly interesting is that in a pair of students, it is not always the same student who provides the help, and often the students will take it in turns to help and encourage each other.

Traffic light key words or phrases starters are an excellent way of showing how learning has to be built on and developed. These work particularly well at higher levels of GCSE or A-level. For example, at the start of a lesson (or series of lessons) on transport across cell membranes, A-level biology students could be presented with a list of all the key terms/phrases that they will encounter in the new topic. They would then be asked to 'traffic light' the key words as follows:

Green – A word/phrase I am fully confident with and understand the meaning of.

Amber – A word/phrase I have heard of before, but I am not fully confident I understand it.

Red – A word/phrase I have never heard of before.

This starter is an excellent way of highlighting both the importance of, and any issues with, prior learning, but also in showing students how learning is a continual upward spiral.

Why can't I answer this exam question? is a good idea for a starter for GCSE or A-level students, but I have seen it successfully used with younger students. This starter works best with a long question, such as a six-mark GCSE question, or a longer A-level question. Often, I would use the same exam question that I would later use to check learning during the lesson's plenary. In most cases, students will usually have some idea of the answer, based on their limited past knowledge, but will almost certainly be unable to answer in anywhere near the depth required to gain the marks on offer. Students may, for example, realise that they require more facts to gain the number of marks than their prior learning has provided, or alternatively, they may be asked to 'explain' something that previously they had only had to 'describe'. Depending on the age and confidence of the students, it is often useful to have a discussion at this stage, as to the nature of their missing learning, e.g. 'So, would just knowing more facts about topic X get you full marks? If not, why not?'

Quite often, when using this idea as a starter, I would go on to get the students to generate their own learning objectives, either individually or as a group for the lesson, which would then enable the question to be answered. So, for example, the students may identify the fact that they need a learning objective, which would provide a balanced number of facts for, and against, a particular argument if they were to be able to 'evaluate' the topic, as the exam question required.

'Why can't I answer this exam question?' starters work particularly well, either if the exam question chosen clearly covers a specific, discrete part of the syllabus, or perhaps when revising a particular topic. They are an excellent way of helping students to appreciate the link between quite precise learning objectives and actual learning outcomes. This can be especially valuable when doing revision lessons with students, where the vast amount of content to be revised can sometimes mean that students lose the ability to break things down into smaller, more manageable sections.

It is often noticeable when using this as a starter idea that it is not only knowledge and understanding that students realise that they are lacking, but perhaps also maths/graphical skills, the ability to interpret a diagram or to balance an argument, etc. These are important, as they help to make students realise that knowledge alone is not always what is required in order to progress in science. Thus, for example, students may realise that a learning objective for the lesson may need to focus on learning how to interpret a particular type of graph, or to be able to correctly calculate a mean, etc.

As with plenaries, I hope that this small range of starters is enough to show that most starter ideas found online, or elsewhere, could very easily be adapted to provide useful feedback on *learning*, as long as this is considered properly at the lesson planning stage.

As with plenaries, the most important thing with a starter that aims to measure learning is that it should give each individual student the chance to demonstrate to *themselves* their previous learning, or lack of it.

1:4 Planning individual lessons – tasks (filling the learning sandwich)

Once you have planned learning objectives with clear success criteria, your plenary to measure the learning achieved during the lesson, and your starter to measure prior, relevant learning at the start of the lesson, then – *and only then* – should you plan your lesson tasks, which will be necessary to achieve the aim of allowing students to successfully complete the plenary and demonstrate their learning.

These tasks may be differentiated, hierarchical, etc. as you wish, but the key thing about planning for learning is that the task should literally 'fill the space' in the lesson between ascertaining the level of learning at the start and at the end of the lesson. It should be one or more of the tasks (*never the plenary*) which are flexible enough to be cut if time pressures mean that something has to be left out of the lesson. If necessary, should your lesson, for example, have three learning objectives, it is *far* better – I would say essential – to complete two of these, and measure the success of those, rather than to plough on and complete all three and not have time to measure the actual learning of any of them. This fact is probably the single, clearest example of why I always insist that whether it is called formative assessment or Assessment for Learning, what I am actually looking at is 'a way of teaching'. Thinking not about 'covering content' or 'getting the teaching done', but instead focusing on what students have actually *learned*. Undoubtedly it is far better to be certain that 66% of the learning has been completed, rather than knowing that 100% of the teaching has been completed, with no clear idea that any actual *learning* has been achieved.

The most important thing about the planned tasks needs to be their *flexibility*. Depending on what is found out from a starter activity, the lesson may need to start with one of a few possible first activities. It may be necessary to have a quick recap of some earlier information or address an important misunderstanding. Alternatively, the starter may show that students' learning is further developed than expected, and perhaps the first activity is no longer needed at all, or it could be reduced. This may sound like 'more work', which I have already said should not be the result of this approach to teaching. However, if learning is seen as a continuum, and tasks for the whole continuum are available (perhaps from earlier or later units, or years, if necessary) then it really should be just the case of making sure that the correct range of tasks is available. With time, this will inevitably become easier, as you become more and more aware of the type of problems that your students are likely to have had with prior learning when covering a particular topic. You will have to trust me on this, although in chapter 6, for your reassurance, I have included some comments by staff who tried these methods for the first time, some of whom were very sceptical, but who found that this approach to planning really was beneficial.

For those who may be thinking at this point that this method of planning and teaching would inevitably mean that content was not fully covered, I agree. Teaching for learning is about *quality*, *not quantity*. I would also suggest if you are concerned by this to consider how much better a student would do in any exam, if they were certain of 66% of their learning, rather than had 'some idea' of 100% of it. Or, to put it another way, what is the point of teaching GCSE level eight or nine work to a student who will only ever gain a level five? Surely it is much more important to ensure that the student is totally confident with all aspects of the work at levels four and five?

I am always amazed at the objections to this approach to teaching. 'But it is not fair if the students don't get the chance to cover everything' or 'What if I end up not covering something which is then in their exam?' To me these arguments are illogical. It would be like teaching somebody to drive by taking them out in a Mini one week, a large van the next week, a tractor the following week, towing a caravan the following week, in an articulated lorry the following week, etc. and then getting them to take their test in a mid-sized family car. After all, they may have to drive one of the others at some point in their life! Clearly this is nonsense, and the learner needs to focus on being able to drive the key vehicle, which they need to demonstrate they have learned enough about driving in. So, why should it be any different with learning science in school? Students should learn what they need to *succeed*, not simply experience things for the sake of it. If you have concerns that this approach will be frowned upon by your senior leaders, one solution might be to use extension work as home-learning tasks.

Finally, it is important to realise that planning for learning should encompass planning of sequences of lessons, not individual lessons.

In the following section, you will see how planning for whole topics or years, using these same principles, will bring about even greater benefits in student progress.

1:5 Planning for learning across a science course

KS3 science in particular is often the ultimate example of teaching – rather than learning – being the centre of long-term science planning. All too often, the KS3 curriculum in science consists of a number of topics, such as cells, light, the periodic table, forces, the human body, etc. each of which, or perhaps each couple of which, are followed by a test. At best, this will be followed by a lesson in which the test is 'gone over' – which usually means the teacher complaining about the lack of work done by the students to prepare for the test, and providing the correct answers! In this way, by the end of the key stage, all the necessary work is 'taught', and in KS4, the staff spend much of their time complaining about the lack of learning done by the students in KS3! The chances are that the process will then be repeated at KS4, and with KS5 teachers! Admit it, this all sounds very familiar!

As with planning individual lessons for learning, the solutions are fairly straightforward, do *not* require any extra workload, and simply change the focus from teaching to learning. Or, as another teacher on the original King's College Project put it, 'Shifting the focus from what the teacher is putting into the process, to what the learner is getting out of it.'

Planning a topic

As with planning lessons for learning, the key thing with planning a topic is to ascertain exactly where students' strengths and weaknesses are *before* starting a unit, in effect, by having a starter to examine relevant prior learning for the whole unit. This may take a whole lesson, or perhaps half of one or less, but it will be time very well spent. Plenaries also need to be planned, which will measure the learning completed for the whole unit, or for part of the unit, and – most importantly – the planning of these plenaries should allow time for any misunderstandings to be addressed. Finally, as with planning lessons for learning, the various tasks to be completed should then be fitted into the available space between these two – more on this later.

By adopting this same approach to topic planning as individual lesson planning, the students will also see that long-term, as well as short-term, goals are all linked to *progress in learning*, rather than the 'coverage of content' which, unfortunately, all too often students seem to associate with science lessons – in a negative way.

Topic starters can be extensions of the type of ideas stated in lesson starters earlier in this chapter. For example, as mentioned, I have used the shared diagrams starter on cells idea (page 33) at both KS4 and KS5 to check the actual learning of students, before embarking on units of work that build on prior learning on 'cells'. Similarly, fishtail diagrams (page 35) and whole lesson discussions (see chapter 2) can produce a wealth of information on prior learning, and can easily take most, or all, of a lesson. The key thing, with using starters like this, is to allow enough time to really get a very good idea of what prior learning the *whole group* is confident with, and especially what prior learning they lack confidence with.

It is worth noting at this point that with well-motivated students, where carrying out home learning tasks is not a major problem (yes, there are some of these!), then preparation home tasks can be done ready for these starter lessons. These may, for example, ask students to do a 3-2-1 type exercise (page 33) on their prior learning on a particular topic or, alternatively, to write a number of definitions, or to traffic light definitions with their confidence, etc. The home tasks could even be presented in the form of a quiz on the previous learning. Tasks done like this, in advance, will not only add to the lesson, but will already prepare the students for the idea that they are going to build on their previous learning. Many of the lesson starter ideas (page 31) can be used partially at home, if possible, although I fully appreciate that this might not always be the case with many students where these tasks would need to be done during a lesson. This is, however, time well spent, rather than just 'ploughing straight in' to the new topic and simply 'hoping for the best'.

One simple topic starter idea that works particularly well in Year 7, where students may arrive at secondary school with a variety of levels of understanding of particular areas of science, is to actually present the 'end of topic' test at the *start* of the unit of work. If this is then marked quickly (although not necessarily with as much detail) by the teacher or through peer marking, this can be invaluable for actually knowing the 'starting position' of the group as a whole. For example, one of my previous Year 7 classes, when doing their end of topic test on 'electricity' in their first lesson of the new unit, showed that they all had a very good understanding of the various basic symbols used in circuits, and knew how to draw simple series circuits. These basic facts seemed very well learned, regardless of the primary schools the students had attended. However, it was also clear that as a group, they had learned little about parallel circuits. In this way, the time used to complete the end of unit test during the 'starter' lesson was made up by not needing to use a lesson revisiting work on basic series circuits and circuit symbols.

This idea of having *flexibility* to cover lessons, or parts of lessons, actually *needed* for student learning when tackling a unit of work, rather than having a 'one size fits all' approach that inevitably focuses on teaching, again highlights why I have said that what I am talking about is 'a way of teaching'.

Another method used to assess former learning – rather than teaching – is to use a list of specification statements that will be covered during the topic. These can be directly taken from examination specifications at higher levels, or they could be a simple list of all the learning aims for the topic. During the starter lesson, the students would self-assess these using traffic lights. (See more on this, and an example, in chapter 5.) It would be stressed to the students that it would be expected that their learning of most of the statements, at this stage, would be 'red'; that is, non-existent. However, by careful inclusion of one or two key statements that revisit earlier work, it is easily possible to judge the students' confidence in their prior learning.

Topic plenaries are essential in order to correctly measure the learning of the students and to discover, *and deal with*, any misconceptions. Depending on the length of the topic, this plenary lesson may come part way through (a longer topic), or just before the end (a shorter topic) or perhaps even both (a very long topic).

As with starter lessons, plenary lessons could involve the same sort of plenary ideas as for single lessons (see page 24). Alternatively, they could involve a mini test or using short-answer or multiple-choice questions to test learning to date. Or the list of topic statements traffic lighted as the topic starter (see above) could be revisited, and students could be asked to look again at their earlier self-assessments and update them accordingly.

What is *absolutely essential* with topic plenaries is that time is available after the plenary in order to address any areas of concern. This could be the remainder of the lesson or a follow-on lesson being used to revisit an area of general concern, or use of structured worksheets, textbooks, etc. to allow students to address individual areas of concern. There could even be opportunities for peer-to-peer teaching.

There may not be time to address all the areas of concern, and it may be necessary for the teacher to make a note of particular problems to be dealt with during revision sessions or towards the end of the year, etc. However, if each lesson in the topic has focused on learning and the evaluation of progress, both by the teacher and the students, then both parties should already have a fairly good idea of which problems, if any, will arise at the plenary stage of a topic. This once more highlights the importance of seeing these formative assessment techniques as a 'whole approach' to teaching, rather than something within lessons.

Topic tasks need to be made available in a much less prescriptive manner than is usually the case in order to complete the whole learning process, rather than dictating that every student should cover subject A during lesson 1, subject B during lesson 2, etc. The tasks for the whole topic or unit of work should be available and be able to be selected as and when necessary. This flexibility is essential if topics are to focus on *student learning*, rather than on *teaching*.

So, in the example of the use of the end of unit test on electricity done by my Year 7 group during their first lesson on the topic mentioned earlier (see page 44), I was able to spend little time on circuit symbols and series circuits, and instead allocate more time on parallel circuits. For another class, even in the same year group, this may not have been the case. By having the flexibility of selection of the appropriate materials, each group can cover work that they *need*, in order to progress their learning. This is a classic example of allowing science teachers to 'step off the hamster wheel'.

Some teachers, at this stage, may be thinking that this would mean that some students would not have time to complete all the tasks in the topic. This is correct, and is exactly as it should be! If student attainment clearly varies across a whole year group, then why on earth should all students be taught all the same information? Where is the logic in that? Trying to shoehorn all the topic content into every individual, or group, is pointless. Carrying on with the Year 7 electricity work, as an example: what would be the point of a low set, with almost no understanding of circuits, symbols, etc. ploughing quickly through series and parallel circuits, leaving them probably confused and lacking proper learning of either? Surely, it is far better to ensure that such a group improves their learning of the basics of circuit symbols and series circuits, and only deals with parallel circuits as far as there is time to do so, or not at all, if time is lacking. Far better for whichever teacher continues their learning in future years to know that all the students at least have a thorough level of learning of circuit symbols and series circuits, and that they are then able to move on from there. This would avoid the 'You were taught series and parallel circuits last year, why don't you know it? Now I am going to have to teach it all again' situation which, unfortunately, happens all too frequently, in *all* three science disciplines.

Clearly, this 'free-choice' method of covering a topic needs some basic structure – anarchy is not being suggested here. So, it may be, for example, that it would be expected that lower sets cover up to at least a certain standard, while higher sets would be expected to cover work up to a different standard. The important thing is that the topic starter should be used to judge *where* learning starts and finishes, for a particular group, and what tasks are required rather than a rigid 'one size fits all' approach.

As with all my experience of formative assessment techniques, this might take some getting used to, but it should *not* involve teachers doing more work. Clearly the same amount of task material would be required as with the more traditional approach of teaching science. The difference would simply be in how the task material is *selected and used* by different teachers, for different teaching groups.

KS3 planning example

Consider a KS3 unit of work, which has eight lessons allocated to it. Usually this would involve six lessons of the students being *taught*, one lesson completing a test, and one lesson 'going over' the test. Below is a general example of how this same topic might be outlined, using this planning for learning approach for a whole unit of work.

Lesson 1* – Topic starter to measure relevant prior learning.

Lessons 2-5 – Most appropriate four tasks selected from a choice of six that develop in terms of level, or complexity, of learning.

Lesson 6* – Plenary on whole topic.

Lesson 7* – Time to deal with any issues arising from topic plenary.

Lesson 8 – End of topic test.

Lesson 9* – Formative use of test (see chapter 5).

*Although there are now nine rather than eight lessons, lessons 1, 6, 7 and 9 may not need a whole lesson for every unit. Thus, across the whole year, this approach to planning topics *does* fit into the same amount of overall time – and has done so, very successfully, in a range of secondary schools.

Summary

What is most important with this approach to topic planning, is that it allows *students* to see clearly that they have *progressed in their learning*, even if, for some, this is only in a few topic areas. Far better for the students to feel totally confident in having moved their learning on, in a few key areas, rather than to have been *taught* a lot of material, and to be lacking confidence in their learning of any of it.

This approach to topic planning will only work well if the teacher, *and the students*, are totally confident in what their actual prior, relevant learning is at the start of the unit, and what a realistic end point of learning is for groups and/or individuals by the end of the unit of work. Making assumptions of prior learning will, undoubtedly, result in lack of success with this approach to planning. As will having unduly false hopes for progress. These are two serious problems in science teaching. Unfortunately, all too often, *prior teaching* is used as a measure of where to move groups on from, rather than *prior learning*.

There may be teachers reading this who will be tempted to say things like, 'My Year X, set Y class never learn anything. So, what would happen with them?' My answer to anybody who is thinking like that is that almost certainly the reason that one particular class seems not to 'learn anything' is because the basic principles of **planning for learning** have been missing from their lessons, and the students are instead used to teachers focusing on teaching.

Finally, I would like to point out that these techniques have been successfully used with every age and ability group, from the very lowest attainers in Year 7, to future vets and medics studying A-level, or the International Baccalaureate in Year 13. No student is ever too low, nor too high, in ability to be able to benefit from having a clear understanding of how their current learning fits into the 'bigger picture', or of what learning is required of them.

Chapter 2
Questions and discussions

2:1 Introduction – I'm a teacher, of course I can run discussions

At its core, science, as a subject, is all about asking questions and looking for answers. So why is it then that in the vast majority of the hundreds of science lessons I have observed, over many years in a wide range of different schools, the 'class discussion' part of the lesson has so often been, by some way, the weakest part?

It never ceases to amaze me that so many teachers feel that all teachers can 'obviously' run discussions with groups of students and similarly, how little focus that this essential skill is given at a practical level with teacher training, in too many cases.

Just one example of this from trainee teachers is when I have been shown lesson plans, sometimes running to several sides of A4 with almost every detail of the lesson meticulously planned – even subdivided at times into 'what the teacher will do' and 'what the students will do' sections – and more often than not, near the start, the end or both, in parts of the lesson plan there will be the word 'discussion' with an allotted time for it. Sometimes, more information will be provided, such as, 'Discussion to check understanding of the first learning objective.' No matter how these lesson plans are worded, the implication is the same; that the discussion will somehow just 'happen', with the teacher in control of it.

For teachers with more experience, lesson plans often contain less, not more, information on these mysterious 'discussions'. When queried about this, the inevitable response is almost always something vague, such as 'I will use a range of questions to find out what the students have actually learned.'

From my experience, discussions are usually by some way the weakest part of science lessons, but it is not just me saying this, because it turns out that there has been plenty of research carried out on oral work in schools. I certainly do not claim to have read any of it, however, ever since the King's College Project, and at various subsequent conferences, I have picked up a number of facts that support my claims. Whenever I came across one of these amazing facts, I always went away and did some simple research of my own, to find out if what I had heard was true. Now I wish to make it clear here that this was not done in any way scientifically, and no statistical analysis of results was carried out. That was never my intention. Instead, I just used the simplest method I could think of to check the facts, concentrating on what actually happens in real science lessons. I can, however, say that each of my 'tests' has been repeated in a variety of secondary schools, across different ages and abilities. Although the findings for each test varied, what was clear was that the underlying conclusion was always the same as the fact that I had originally been presented with.

In the following section I will not only look at some of the most startling facts I have picked up over the years on just how poor discussions in science lessons are, but I will also explain some simple ways to check these in your school's science lessons.

2:2 Key facts about discussions in schools and how to test them

What students retain

According to Edgar Dale, an American educator (OK, I admit, I had never heard of him either), an average student will retain:

- 10% of what they read

- 20% of what they hear
- 30% of what they see
- 50% of what they see and hear
- **70% of what they say and write**
- 90% of what they say as they do.[1]

Obviously the details of the figures here are not important, but it clearly shows the power of students being involved in a discussion. So, what do we know about classroom discussions?

Teachers dominate discussions

At one conference I attended it was mentioned that teachers usually dominate 70-90% of lessons.[2] But do science teachers really dominate science lessons and discussions to this degree? Should you feel that this imbalance does not occur in science discussions in your school, then I would suggest that the next time you have an opportunity to observe a science lesson, you use two stop clocks, and switch one on each time the teacher speaks to the class, and the other stop clock each time that students speak (speaking officially – not just chatter while 'working'). You could even use the two stop clocks to specifically look at the balance of teacher and student input during the planned discussions. Whether you get these exact figures of 70-90% or not, one thing is guaranteed; in far too many science lessons, the balance will be hugely in favour of the teacher speaking most, as I have found out for myself using exactly this method on many occasions.

An interesting aside here is that whenever I have done this, even when presented with the evidence of the figures from the two stop clocks, most teachers have disputed the findings, and insisted that there must have been a mistake. It seems that not only do science teachers like to dominate lessons, and in particular, discussions, but they do so often, without even being aware that they are!

---

1   Anderson, H. M. *Dale's cone of experience*. Available at: www.queensu.
.   ca/teachingandlearning/modules/active/documents/Dales_Cone_of_
     Experience_summary.pdf (Accessed: 9 November 2021).

2   Cook, V. (2000) *Second language learning and language teaching*. Beijing:
     Foreign Language Teaching and Research Press.

The silent many

Another fact that I came across over the years is that apparently 60% of secondary school students never have a conversation with an adult on any one day at school.[3]

Now again, it is not the detail of this fact that concerns me but the accuracy of the idea behind it with regard to science lessons. Is it really true that more than half of the students say nothing to the teacher during a science lesson? As before this can be fairly easily checked during a lesson observation. One way in which I have done this, is to use a seating plan of the students, and simply tick by each name when a student makes an oral contribution to the lesson. One thing that this will undoubtedly confirm, is that all too frequently, especially in larger groups, well over half of the students will not actually contribute at all. So, the 'silent few' are in fact, more often, the 'silent many'.

As an aside at this point, the method used above to focus on which students are responding can also be used to investigate other simple matters, such as: does the teacher subconsciously favour one gender? Does the teacher subconsciously favour a particular area of the room – students on the front or rear desks? Does the teacher subconsciously favour those who call out? etc. The chances are that whatever the focus of the evidence gathering, it will be clear that a so-called 'class discussion' will actually involve quite a small proportion of the class on, unfortunately, too many occasions.

Short responses

Another fact that I picked up at some point, and looked into, is that apparently the average length of response of a secondary school student to a question is five words.[4] If so, then this would clearly not be of much value in demonstrating their level of learning during a discussion.

The shortness of student responses can be checked quite easily, by using a similar idea to the one above, involving a seating plan of the students. I usually used a simple three-tier 'measure' of responses from the students:

---

3   West-Burnham, J. and Coates, M. (2006) *Transforming education for every child: A practical handbook*. Stafford: Network Continuum Education Press.

4   Ibid.

Tier 1 was a short-answer response, a single word or phrase, or very short statement, e.g. 'Photosynthesis', 'Unbalanced forces' or 'They are all non-metals'. The type of answer that would gain only a single mark in a test or exam.

Tier 2 was a longer sentence or possibly a short explanation, e.g. 'The arrows show the direction the energy flows in a food chain' or 'Alpha radiation is weakest, as paper stopped it.' The type of answer that would gain two marks in a test or exam.

Tier 3 was used for longer responses of more than one sentence, usually with some more detailed reasoning or explanation, e.g. 'Herbivores have eyes at the sides of their heads. This gives them a wider field of vision, so they can see potential predators' or 'If magnesium is more reactive than copper, then the magnesium would displace the copper, producing solid copper and magnesium sulphate.' This is the type of answer that might be awarded three, or even four, marks in a test or exam. It would be very unusual for a student to answer with something much longer than this, but if they did, I might add a tier 4.

You can see that this method is far from scientific, and gives only a rough approximation of the type of responses that students give. However, having tried this on several occasions, in most cases it is usually seen that most answers tend to fall into tier 1, with a few in tier 2, and even fewer, and often none, in tier 3.

Although not positive proof of the 'five word' fact, this does highlight that too many responses in science discussions are far too short to give a really good indication to either the teacher, or the student, of actual *learning*.

Wait times

My favourite fact about discussions was one that Dylan Wiliam introduced me to, right back in the early days of the King's College Assessment Project. At the time, its impact on me was huge, and it remained so for the rest of my career. Apparently, the average wait time between a teacher asking a question and then adding to it with another follow-on statement, or other form of 'encouragement' is... 0.9 seconds.[5] That's right folks, the average teacher waits for *less than*

---

5   Rowe, M. B. (1972) 'Wait-time and rewards as instructional variables: Their influence on language, logic, and fate control.' *Journal of Research in Science Teaching*, 11: pp. 81-94.

a second between finishing what they have asked their students and starting to talk again! And yet so many teachers wonder why so few students join in their 'discussions'!

When Dylan first mentioned this fact I was astounded, as I am to this day. The next time I observed a colleague teaching, I sat with my stop clock and timed his 'wait times' between asking a question and starting to say something else, to trigger a response. The colleague I was observing was an outstanding science teacher, who was himself also involved in The King's College Project, so he too had heard Dylan's information. However, even he had wait times that were often too short to time accurately on a stop clock, and that never ran to more than two seconds. Overall, I found that his wait times averaged only just over a second.

This is a very easy fact to check, and as with the others, it is not the detail that I think is important, but the overall message. If, during an observation, you use a stopwatch to check wait times regardless of the accuracy or figures, one thing is fairly certain: you will find that wait times are definitely less than the teacher will estimate for themselves. Most teachers feel like they wait for several seconds, when in reality, this is very rarely the case. Science teachers, I have to say, are particularly bad at this; too quickly adding additional information or clues to 'help' or 'steer' the answers. So for example, a teacher will ask students, 'Do you remember the chemical used to do photosynthesis?' but will very quickly follow this with a clue, such as, 'It sounds like the chemical used in swimming pools.' The reason for this approach is often due to the fear that they will not be able to 'teach' all the knowledge they need to unless they move through the discussion quickly. Again, the emphasis being on teaching, *not learning*.

I am sure there are many more key facts about classroom discussions that you could find with a bit of research, but these are the ones that I have taken on board over the years. They illustrate extremely well some of the big problems with 'discussions' in science. This is why using class discussions as a starter or plenary exercise is often less than successful as a method of measuring prior learning.

My aim for the rest of this chapter is to deal with these problems, and look at how to improve the usefulness of class discussions as methods for *measuring learning*.

2:3 The purposes of classroom discussions

Before getting into the techniques for improving classroom discussions in science, I think it is only fair that I explain what I feel are the key purposes of such discussions. Now I know I said this book would not be theoretical, but I consider this less as 'theory' and more a chance to have a little thinking time.

So, you are a science teacher and your purpose of having a discussion is… to check knowledge and understanding obviously. But is that really all? Time to have a cup of coffee and give this some more thought. Clearly checking prior learning is important, but what does 'prior' mean? During the present lesson? Recent lessons? Lessons from the previous year? Lessons from the previous key stage? Lessons from the previous school? Already, simply *checking prior learning* alone can open up a range of possible purposes for a particular discussion.

However, is checking prior learning really all you hope to get from your discussion? What about getting the students interested in and motivated by science? Surely you would want to interest and motivate your students by what they hear during the discussion? Not only would this be useful for their long-term learning, but there is plenty of evidence to show that behaviour is improved if students are interested and well motivated. So, this too, would need to be included in the purpose of classroom discussions.

If you reread the previous paragraph, you will notice that it mentioned 'what they hear during the discussion'. Not every student can contribute verbally to every classroom discussion, but obviously it is extremely important that students listen to what others have to say. Therefore, it follows that another key purpose of a discussion is to *improve the listening skills* of the students.

While the students are listening to their peers and contributing to the discussion, is it not also important that they are actually thinking about what they say or hear? After all, surely the most important ever science question is 'Why?' It must surely follow then, that a discussion should encourage students to think. But how do we know if a student is thinking, or thinking at the correct level required? One way of extending thinking is to use Bloom's taxonomy.[6] For those who are

6   Armstrong, P. (2010) *Bloom's taxonomy*. Available at: https://cft.vanderbilt.edu/guides-sub-pages/blooms-taxonomy/ (Accessed: 24 November 2021).

new to this, it is basically a simple way of categorising educational goals, including extending thinking, that build on their predecessors. (See list below.) Many teachers have been led to believe that this is a hierarchical structure, which is not how many educationalists now interpret it. However, it is clear that science discussions should be used to encourage and develop thinking from basic recall through to evaluating and creating.

- Remember
- Understand
- Apply
- Analyse
- Evaluate
- Create

Already it is clear that the purpose of a science discussion should be for much more than simply 'finding out what students know'. There is one more purpose that I think you may be unlikely to have considered. That is the idea of developing metacognition. At this point, I can almost imagine those with the last of their cup of coffee left have almost spilt it. 'Developing what?' I hear you say, 'No way are my Year 9s going to be doing any of that on a Friday afternoon.' Well, here I disagree. Metacognition, in this context, is about getting students to think about their learning. This could be as simple as encouraging them to consider how confident they are with a particular concept, or asking them to evaluate a range of different learning techniques used in a particular lesson. For example, 'Did the explanation in the textbook, or the practical, best help you to understand…?'

At higher levels, metacognition may involve students *evaluating* their own learning, in terms of what they might have done differently in their approach to the learning, rather than to the tasks. For example, 'If you could spend an extra 10 minutes on this work, what might you do to improve your learning of …?' At whatever level, it is important to remember that for the students the learning itself should *not* be the only goal.

Hopefully now you will see that a good classroom discussion in science should be considering all of these purposes. I believe that, unfortunately, through no fault of their own, too many science teachers give too little thought to this range of purposes, particularly when 'planning' discussions, often with only knowledge and basic recall being their focus.

2:4 So, what does a really good science discussion need?

In order to cover most, or all, of the key purposes of the discussion listed above, I think that a high-quality, useful science discussion would need the following three things. All three of these will be looked at in much greater detail starting on page 60. For the moment the key points are:

Planning

A discussion that is going to serve the key purposes of informing both teacher *and students* of learning will undoubtedly need to have questions, and probably potential answers, carefully planned in advance. As a teacher, it is important to consider what you would expect to hear if the students had, or had not, learned what was expected of them.

This level of planning is so much more than just 'having some ideas of some questions'. Planning a discussion should be tackled in much the same way as planning any other lesson, or part of a lesson, with thought given to differentiation, inclusion, sequencing, etc. Planning is so important to good science discussions that I have dedicated a large part of the rest of this chapter to it, starting on page 60.

Feedback

Clearly, one of the most important aspects of a discussion that aims to inform on learning is the feedback that the discussion provides. This will be *feedback* both to the teacher *and* to the students. In particular, information about misunderstandings or problems with recall or concepts should be of great importance, not least because for the teacher these should be vital in adapting the remainder of the lesson, or future lessons, if necessary.

Involvement

If a teacher is going to be aware of all (or at least most) of the students' learning and the students, as individuals, are going to be aware of their own learning, so it follows that a high-quality discussion should target the involvement of all (or most) of the students. Unfortunately, too often classroom discussions in science are dominated by a few individuals, with too many students taking the easy way out, and simply not contributing at all (see pages 51-52). As with planning, this is an area of discussion work that I think is too rarely considered during teacher training, with the result that many science teachers do not readily have the skills to employ to alter this situation and get more students involved. Hopefully, the ideas that start on page 68 will help to at least go some way to addressing this situation.

So, there we have it. For a high-quality classroom discussion in science, all you need is: to plan all the possible questions, and potential answers; to ensure that the teacher and the students get useful feedback on their learning; and get all the students involved. Easy, eh? Clearly not. So, is it any wonder that discussions are so often the weakest part of a science teacher's repertoire? The good news, however, is as with all work on AfL, I honestly feel that improving the quality of discussions does *not* involve a great deal of work. There is no doubt that it will initially involve *some* extra work, although instead of 'extra' I really feel that the word 'different' could be applied. This new approach to discussions, however, will also include the benefit that it will remove other work, often produced as a result of poor-quality discussions and failure to address the three key points discussed above.

2:5 The typical science discussion

I have observed many, many science discussions over the years, and unfortunately, the vast majority of these are poor at providing any real indication of *learning* by students. Instead, they tend to focus on recall of knowledge and facts, which too many science teachers seem to think are indicators of learning. Looking at Bloom's taxonomy above (page 56), it is clear that such recall is only associated with one of the phrases on Bloom's taxonomy, which makes me wonder, is this really all we are aiming for?

However, all too often, things are actually worse than even this might suggest. Checking recall of facts and knowledge usually involves the use of short-answer questions, which in turn involve only a very small proportion of the students: often the loudest, often in a mixed-gender setting, boys, the most confident, or even those in particular areas of the room. Even allowing for the very low level of information gleaned from such questions, the result is that the discussion provides feedback on learning of, and to, only a small proportion of the students.

Another problem that I have often observed during discussions is the fact that science teachers are usually very conscious of time constraints within their lessons. So, in order to allow time for a practical activity, they will hurry along the discussion at the start of the lesson in many ways. This can be by deliberately targeting students, who they know will give the correct answer, or by providing clues. So, the question 'What did all the group one metals share in common?' if not quickly, and correctly, answered, will often be followed by a clue, such as, 'Remember what happened when we put each of them in water last lesson.' This 'hurrying on' of discussions inevitably leads to them being of little, if any, use as a feedback tool for learning, instead simply allowing the teacher to 'tick the box' saying they 'did a discussion' at the start of a lesson.

Another typical problem during science discussions is the lack of thinking time allowed for the students. This follows on from the perceived need to hurry discussions, to allow time for the 'real work', or perhaps so that home learning can be recorded, etc. I have actually heard science teachers say, on more than one occasion, that they need to 'get through these questions quickly, as there is a lot to do today'. Clearly implying that the 'lot to do' is important and, by inference, that the discussion is less important!

The other reason thinking time is often lacking, however, is that the questions are often of such low demand that the teacher, rightly, feels that little time should be needed to recall the answer.

So, unfortunately, most of the science discussions I have witnessed over the years have been far from the ideal of meeting the three key criteria: well planned, providing useful feedback on learning, and getting as many students as possible involved. You may feel that this is a somewhat harsh assessment of my fellow science teachers, and there are undoubtedly many science teachers who run very good, or even truly outstanding, class discussions. However, I would challenge anybody who feels upset by my statement to read this whole chapter, then go and observe a number of different science teachers, with different ages and abilities of students, and not to come to the same conclusion that I have done. During my many years of observations, I have found that all too often the general standard of science discussions is often not very good. Sorry.

2:6 Planning a good AfL discussion

There is no doubt at all that the first step in planning a good science discussion that will provide useful feedback on learning is to plan some really good-quality questions. I mentioned at the start of this chapter how rarely this seems to be covered, specifically during teacher training, which considering its importance I find perplexing.

Better questions produce better discussions

Wow, I can hear you saying to yourself, how revolutionary! This book was clearly worth the investment of my money and/or time. Clearly, this does not sound anything other than totally obvious, so let me turn this around and pose a few questions for you, as a fellow science teacher, to think on:

- When was the last time that you saved a presentation (PowerPoint, Smartboard, etc.) into a shared area for others in your department to use?

- When was the last time that you saved a worksheet (Workbook, task sheet, test, etc.) into a shared area for others in your department to use?

- Finally, when was the last time that you saved a good discussion question into a shared area for others in your department to use?

Hopefully from this you will see what I am getting at. Teachers all know that better questions lead to better discussions, but they do not *prioritise planning and sharing* of questions in the same way that they plan and share other resources. Why not? It seems blindingly obvious to me that the planning and sharing of questions for discussion should be given equal standing to other types of planning, yet this is very rarely the case.

As I mentioned earlier, too many questions in science discussions seem to involve very simple recall of knowledge and information, but it does not take much to change these questions into ones that will allow a much more informative discussion, both for the teacher and the students. Here are three very simple examples that, with small modifications, will provide far greater information on learning to both teacher and students:

Typical question 1: *What usually has valves: arteries or veins?*

This same information can be checked, along with a much deeper understanding of the students' *learning* on arteries, veins and the role of valves, by altering the question just slightly...

Better question 1: *Why is it that veins are more likely than arteries to have valves?*

Just the small alteration in the planning of this question has altered it to provide a huge amount of additional information on prior learning.

Typical question 2: *Javid said 'atoms or molecules', but which word is right?*

Again, a much deeper understanding of the students' learning on particles could be gleaned by altering this question slightly...

Better question 2: *Explain why it might matter which word Javid uses when he said both 'atoms' and 'molecules' in his answer.*

No longer is this a simple guessing game for the students to get the right answer, but a probe into their understanding of the difference between atoms and molecules.

Typical question 3: *What are the ends of a magnet called?*

This will often be followed with another simple recall question on which poles attract and which repel. But a far greater insight into the understanding of magnetic poles and their nature, and the learning of students in this area, could be unlocked by altering the question slightly...

Better question 3: *What might happen if we cut a magnet in half?* (Or into three pieces, if you want to challenge higher attaining students.)

This will demonstrate, at a much deeper level, the students' understanding of the concept of magnetic poles – even if their answers are not actually correct.

In each of these cases, by altering the question slightly, a simple 'closed' question and answer session has been opened up, to allow students to demonstrate, both to the teacher *and themselves*, their actual level of learning of a small topic. Using more open-ended questions also naturally moves you 'further up' Bloom's taxonomy.

These more productive questions are extremely unlikely just to 'come to mind' in the heat of a lesson, without either some careful planning in advance or after using such questions on many occasions. So, if a science teacher relies on running a discussion without any prior planning of questions then more often than not, it will be the typical, simplistic questions that spring to mind. Rare would be the science teacher who, in the heat of the classroom, faced with a busy lesson to get through and students displaying various behavioural needs, would be able to just pull questions like the improved versions above from the top of their head.

Planning more thought-provoking questions in advance will undoubtedly sound like more work. However, look again at the three questions above. How much discussion time would be filled with the original three questions, compared with the improved versions? If these improved questions were also saved and shared, like other scientific resources for others in the department to use, then even *less* planning time would be required.

As a science teacher, one of the easiest places to start in planning these more thought-provoking and informative questions, is to use something called **the Q-Matrix**.

Using the Q-Matrix

I would like to make it abundantly clear that in no way am I laying claim to this super-useful tool, which I believe is generally attributed to Chuck Wiederhold.[7] However, this is an excellent starting point for improving discussions. Here is the version of the Q-Matrix that I use.

---

7   Wiederhold, C. (1995) *Cooperative learning and higher level thinking: The Q-Matrix*. San Clemente, CA: Kagan Publishing.

	is	did	can	would	will	might
Why						
How						
When						
Where						
What						
Who						

When using the Q-Matrix, as you move up the arrow, questions become more thought-provoking and higher in order of thinking. So, a question starting with 'Who is...' or 'What did...' would equate on Bloom's taxonomy (see page 56) to the very lowest 'remember' level, whereas asking a question that starts with 'Why might...' is more likely to equate to Bloom's taxonomy 'levels' of 'analyse' or 'evaluate'. Question stems that start in the shaded area are likely to provide a lot more information on learning.

One way of checking your understanding of this tool might be to look back at the three typical and improved questions used as examples above, and see how their question stems fit into the Q-Matrix. As a basic starting point to developing better questions, the Q-Matrix is an invaluable planning tool. However, as was mentioned earlier, there is much more to a really successful science discussion than simply having good-quality questions.

One thing that needs to be considered at the planning stage is potential answers and what you, as a teacher, might do with them. Let's use the question on veins, arteries and valves from earlier to look at this. The original question was very low level, and simply asked, 'What usually has valves: arteries or veins?' Clearly, the nature of this question means that any student, even with no prior knowledge of this topic, has a 50% chance of getting it right. Obviously if most students get the answer wrong the teacher would know to address this topic. In practice, what tends to happen with this type of question is that the science teacher will get responses from the most vocal or confident students, who will either know the information or guess correctly. The teacher will then assume the class has learned this fact and move on. But what about those who did not answer? Or those students who got the answer right by guessing? Or those who simply waited and copied their peers, whom they see as smarter?

Looking at the higher-level version of this question – 'Why is it that veins are more likely than arteries to have valves?' – clearly the range of potential answers is much wider, which obviously means so too could be the number of students involved in providing an answer, getting more students directly involved in the discussion. A student is also not going to be able to guess an answer to this question. Already this improved question has the possibility to discover more about the learning of a wider range of students on this particular topic point.

This brings up the important point of *why* the question is being asked. What does the teacher actually want to find out from this part of the discussion? I have often been surprised when I have asked science teachers, 'What were you trying to find out when you asked...?' Unfortunately many of these teachers are unable to state clearly what their intention was, other than a vague, 'To check the students' understanding.'

For example, let's delve deeper into the higher-level question, 'Why is it that veins are more likely than arteries to have valves?' The question could be asked to check the understanding of the difference in blood pressures in the two types of blood vessels. Alternatively, it could be used to check the understanding of the fact that many more veins than arteries carry blood against gravity. Depending on the reasons the question is actually being asked, it is vital to be aware of the possible 'right' and 'wrong' answers that may come up. Ideally, at this planning stage, thought will also be given as to what to actually do if students have misconceptions about any aspects of the key *learning*.

This does not mean that during planning the teacher needs to make a list, or even attempt to think of, every possible answer to a question, but the key point is that you should know what *type* of things you would expect to hear if the students had – or had not – learned a basic concept behind your question.

This means, therefore, that when using the Q-Matrix to generate more informative questions as part of the planning, thought needs to be given to precisely what knowledge, concepts and learning the question is being used to demonstrate understanding of, and what would be the key triggers to suggest this had successfully been achieved (or not). This is very much like the idea of lesson objective success criteria discussed in chapter 1. When planning questions for a discussion, the teacher should have an idea what 'success' would be.

Where next?

It follows on from the idea of planning questions to show deeper understanding, and considering possible outcomes, that at the planning stage the teacher also needs to consider what they might say/do next if the desired learning is, or is not, being demonstrated adequately. Again, this does not mean that a discussion needs to be planned at the level of detail so that 'if students say ..., then I will say ...' for every possible answer. But it is important to know the main pathways your discussion might take. In general terms this means planning outcomes, such as, 'If the students do show understanding of ... then we can move on to ..., whereas, if the students lack understanding of ..., then I will need to move back, or sideways, to ...', etc.

When I have mentioned this to science teachers in the past, there have been occasions when the response has been that there would be a large number of these 'possible outcomes' in a discussion. However, a good discussion that aims to check learning should only be checking on a small number of key facts, concepts, etc. so the possible choices here should be limited. I think the issue that these teachers highlighted was linked more to their previous ideas of using a discussion to check the recall of many different facts – using lots of short-answer questions. As I have, hopefully, made clear by now, this is *not* what a proper science discussion to monitor *learning* should be.

Saving and sharing questions

The final part of the planning for discussions should be the saving and sharing of questions that work well with departmental colleagues. This needs to become just as much a part of the saving of resources, and as natural to do, as the saving and sharing of lesson presentations, worksheets, etc. For example, the third question that I used as an example on page 62, 'What might happen if we cut a magnet in half?' was one that I observed an outstanding NQT use many years ago. After the lesson, I immediately encouraged her to save it, both for herself and in the science shared area on the school's computers. I am certain that this one, inspirational question that probably occurred on the spur of the moment, has since been used by many teachers as a result of this; yet may otherwise have been lost. In this way banks of questions that allow really informative science discussions that help to *measure learning* will build up, and be available for the whole department. Not only will this resource help to maintain a more *consistent* standard of class discussions across the science department, but, as with all shared resources, it will inevitably *reduce the time* that individual teachers have to spend on planning. So, definitely not 'more work'.

2:7 Student involvement in discussions

As mentioned earlier, a useful class discussion to provide formative feedback on learning, to both students and the teacher, clearly needs to involve the majority, and ideally all, of the students participating. Many times, when I have mentioned this to science teachers, they immediately say that there is not time enough to get all of the students involved. So, what often tends to happen is that certain students, considered to be 'indicators' for the group, are targeted with questions. In this way these 'indicator students' are used to 'judge the learning' of the whole group. Alternatively, different students might be targeted during different discussions, on different topics; using the idea that in this way over a few lessons all the students would have had an opportunity to answer.

The problem with these methods is that by the very nature of them, too many students are 'left out', and do not feel that they are part of the discussion. Students are also very smart at picking up on who is, and who is not, likely to be targeted if the 'indicator student' technique is used. Another thing to consider is that with any method that involves careful 'steering' towards individuals in this way, it inevitably leads to the teacher being the person who speaks most during the discussion. Finally, 'steering' of the discussion, by using this technique, also tends to encourage the teacher to 'steer' students towards the answers that they hope to hear.

However, far more important than any of these issues with using these techniques is that the discussion will *not* provide the best feedback on the learning of the *group*, neither to the teacher nor, more importantly, to many of the students.

For those teachers who say that there is not enough time to get all, or most, of the students involved in a discussion, I would suggest the two stop clocks idea mentioned earlier, where an observer records the time that students and the teacher each spend speaking during a discussion. I can almost guarantee that if this is done, it will inevitably show that much more time would be available for more students to contribute, and therefore be judged, if only the teacher said less.

The other challenge that is inevitably raised by science teachers when I suggest that they need to get all their students involved in their classroom discussions is, 'But I have a lot of students who are shy, etc. and who won't contribute.' This is often said as if it is a problem unique to the actual teacher, when obviously every science group, no matter which age or level of attainment, will inevitably have students who do not like to take part in a discussion as much as some other students. What surprises me, however, is how readily so many teachers seem to simply accept that the class discussion is a part of the lesson where certain students can basically opt out and not have to do anything. These same teachers would be unhappy with any student who did not do practical or written tasks, yet they seem not to have this same attitude towards the class discussion. Is it any wonder, therefore, that the students themselves do not see the discussions as important parts of the lesson?

Before looking at some methods for increasing *student involvement* in discussion, I feel that I need to clarify what I mean by the phrase 'student involvement'. I fully understand that it is not possible for every student to make multiple, or perhaps not even single, contributions, during a discussion. However, that does not mean that *all* the students should not be 'involved' in the discussion. What the aim should be is best summed up by a phrase that Christine Harrison used, when giving me feedback on one of my lessons many years ago, during my early work with King's College. When talking about the plenary discussion, she said there had been an 'edge-of-the-seat' atmosphere with all of the students. This is what I mean by having *all* the students involved.

Generating a situation whereby every student is genuinely interested in the discussion – listening carefully, and thinking about what is said even if they, as individuals, may not get the chance to actually contribute verbally. The important point is that every student would be ready to participate. As I type this, I can already imagine some science teachers thinking to themselves, 'Well, he obviously doesn't know my Year 9 or Year 11 class.' The fact is I do. I know exactly what it is like to have a class of unmotivated, poorly behaved individuals, but that is *not* an excuse for not being able to generate an 'edge-of-the-seat' atmosphere during a science discussion. So, how do you get that atmosphere with a group of students?

The following is a range of techniques, all of which will help. The more of them that are used, the better. No one idea (or even all of the ideas) is a magic bullet that will suddenly have all of your students happily contributing to lessons, but all of these techniques will help to encourage greater participation, both verbally and aurally – *actively listening* to other students is a big area of class discussions that is often neglected. In my mind, a successful classroom discussion will have as many students as possible verbally contributing, and those who do not will be actively listening to their peers, and ready to respond to what they hear if asked to do so. Together, this will provide the illusive 'edge-of-the-seat' atmosphere. As with all teaching, these techniques will need practising, by both the teacher and the students, but they will definitely improve the overall quality of science discussions as a learning experience, for the teacher and students alike.

2:8 Methods for getting more students involved

Telling students that the discussion is important

One of the first things that will definitely get more students involved with a discussion is to tell them, before the discussion starts, the *importance* of the discussion. Whenever I have said this to science teachers, they have always seemed somewhat surprised. However, those same teachers are very used to telling their students that a particular practical is important because it 'comes up in the exams', or that a particular diagram is essential to learn because it 'summarises key facts needed later for a test', etc. So, why not tell students that the discussion is important? Too often, too many students see a discussion, especially those used during a starter or a plenary, as unimportant because they are not part of the 'real learning'. These feelings are often subconsciously reinforced by the science teacher, as has already been mentioned. For this reason, students often 'opt out', and do not pay attention or offer answers. But if you not only *tell* students that a discussion is important, but also *justify* this, you will have already altered their mindset towards the discussion, and as a result, you will improve student 'involvement'.

With a discussion used as a starter, I would usually say to students something like, 'This discussion is going to be useful to you, to check if you do really understand the work we learned in the previous lesson/ topic on … and it will then allow us to move on to …' Or perhaps even a more light-hearted version, such as, 'This discussion is important because it will let you find out just how much of all that amazing stuff you learned on … last lesson/unit has fallen out of your brain, while you have been sleeping since then. If we don't check, we might not be ready to move on to …' In both of these cases, the students have already been given a clear purpose for the discussion that too often the teacher will keep to themselves – often assuming that the students can 'obviously tell' what the discussion is for. (A good general tip for new teachers – always work on the assumption that at least some of your students will never have a clue why you are doing what you're doing!) Even worse are those teachers who think that it is not important for the students to actually know what the discussion is for.

As a focus for a discussion, this is so much better than the more traditional science starter of 'Who can remember what we did last lesson?' Recognise that one?

With a plenary discussion, I might say something like, 'We are now going to finish up with an important discussion that will allow you to consider just how well you have learned today's work on …' or 'This discussion is important, as it will help you to decide which of today's learning objectives you have really mastered.' As before, these sentences make it clear to the students that although the lesson tasks have been completed, the discussion that will follow is also an important part of their learning.

Just using the word 'important' when introducing the discussion rather than simply 'launching in' will help get more students' minds focused on the discussion. It sounds too simplistic, but trust me, you will notice a difference when you try it.

It's worth mentioning here that it is vital that having said that the discussion is important, that the teacher then reinforces this too. For example, if a student is not paying attention, remind them of the importance of why they should be paying attention, or say something like, 'We only have 10 minutes to do this discussion, so it is *important* that we make the most of it.' If it is a plenary discussion and the teacher allows students to start packing up their bags, this does *not* show the students that the discussion is important.

Telling the students expectations from the discussion

If ever you are observing lessons in science, it is always worth asking students after they have had a discussion what they were expected to get from the discussion. If you are very lucky, you may get a vague answer, such as 'To check our previous knowledge' or 'To check if we learned today's work.' I would suggest that it would be very rare if a student said anything more precise. Yet, if you ask the same students about other parts of the lesson and what they were expected to get from them, almost always you will receive much more informative answers.

Having told students that the upcoming discussion is *important*, I would try, wherever possible, to tell them what they are *expected* to be able to do at the end of the discussion. For example, with a discussion used as a starter, I might say that it was important as it was going to check prior understanding, but I would usually add something like, 'And at the end of the discussion, you should be able to say/write down the two most important pieces of information that would help with exam questions on this topic.' Alternatively, I may add to the importance of the discussion by saying, 'After the discussion you should be able to list at least four key words that you learned before that will be useful in today's lesson.' Here again, the students' mindset is being altered from the starter discussion being something that they can choose to 'opt out' of, to a discussion that will not only remind them of prior learning, but provide useful information for the *learning* in the rest of the lesson.

With a plenary discussion, I may add to the message of its importance by saying, 'After the discussion, I want you to make a note of one thing that you realised you were a bit confused about, with today's learning on ...' In this case, as things were discussed, I may write key words or phrases on the board for lower attaining students, for them to see throughout the discussion. Alternatively, with a plenary, I may say to the students that, 'After the discussion, I will ask you to traffic light your confidence with today's learning objectives.'

Having a clear and precise goal for what the students, as individuals, need to *achieve* from an upcoming discussion, will inevitably mean that students see the discussion as part of the 'real learning' and not just the bit where 'the teacher and some students talk'. The more precise the prior expectations are, the more students will 'buy in', and become part of the discussion. I guarantee, that this *will* alter the way in which students focus on the discussion.

The combination of telling students that a discussion is important and that there are outcomes that they, as individuals, are expected to get from it, will definitely start towards the illusive 'edge-of-the-seat' atmosphere during science discussions. I am not saying that these will cause every single student to focus or want to participate, but they will generate a totally different attitude. Once I even heard a student turn to his chatty friend during the discussion and say, 'Shhh! I have only got two of the key words, and I need to hear the last one.' Even if this student had not contributed verbally to the discussion, they were clearly an 'active participant'.

Random selection of students

Another key point in a good science discussion to *measure learning*, is to do away with students volunteering answers by putting up hands or calling out, and having a system to select those students to answer 'randomly'. This can be completely random by using a simple random name generator on a PowerPoint presentation or an app (yes, there are apps that do this for you), or by using lolly sticks, etc. with names on. There are many methods for fully random selection of names. Depending on the group size, make-up, etc. names selected once may, or may not, be open to selection again. Generally, it is better to allow student names to be selected more than once, to avoid the 'I've done my turn' feeling spreading.

However, random selection of students to contribute does *not* have to involve the whole class, all of the time. Selection by asking for 'somebody who has a birthday this term' for example, or 'somebody who came to school on a bus' can mean that a *range* of students can be selected at the same time, and then this subgroup can be used before moving on to a different subgroup. By their very nature these groups, if large enough, will provide an adequate cross-section of the whole class, and will form a good indicator of whole-class learning. These subgroups, by their random nature, are more likely to contain a range of attainment levels, than if the teacher selects those who they think produce a range.

I would often start a discussion by asking an apparently random question, such as, 'Who owns a pet that is something other than furry?' By taking a quick visual note of all those who put hands up, I would then follow up by asking each of this subgroup for a response during the science discussion, before moving to the rest of the class. This method provides a random sample from the whole class, and valuable information on the levels of learning of the whole group. Questions such as, 'If you could, who would like to visit the moon?', 'If you could drive a racing car on a track today, who would fancy a go?' or 'If you could meet any of the judges from *Strictly Come Dancing*, who would choose Craig?' have all been used with great success, and have also lightened the atmosphere at the start of a discussion. One particular benefit of this seems to be that the more bizarre the initial question, the more likely students seem to respond. Often students who are usually reluctant to join in discussions seem less reticent to do so when the selection question is something quite odd.

Having students in subgroups does not mean that only one subgroup has to be the sole focus. For example, with the *Strictly Come Dancing* question above, I may ask the first question to those who selected Motsi for the first response, but then move to those who chose Craig for the second question, and so on. Making the selection of the subgroups random further adds to the students as a whole having to be prepared to be involved.

You may worry that as a teacher you would not remember all the students who had selected to be in a particular subgroup, or that some students may simply not volunteer themselves for any subgroup. Undoubtedly, as a teacher, you will find that you improve on this over time – indeed, there are fewer students to focus on than with the whole group. However, there are a couple of other things that will also help you in these circumstances. Firstly, with regards to remembering which students are in which subgroups, you will almost always find that other students in the class inform on their friends: 'Priya, you were in that group' or 'Didn't you say you came to school by car today, Mason?' will become common place. Students, it seems, love to ensure that their 'friends' don't miss out.

As for students who may not volunteer for any group, these are likely to be a small number who the teacher will already be well aware of. Rather than accusing them of not volunteering for a subgroup, I would usually blame myself when addressing such a student, and might say, 'I'm sorry Keira, I can't remember if you said you came on a bus or not, but can you answer this one please?' By using this approach, not only does Keira (and other students) learn that not volunteering an answer is pointless, as she (they) may be asked to contribute anyway, but it also removes any stigma from Keira for not volunteering.

Randomly selecting students to be involved in a discussion is invaluable in building the levels of expectation with students, either the whole group or with subsets. It means that students can no longer sit back and opt out or leave it all to somebody else.

It is important to ensure that other students not in the randomly selected group do not feel that they can just sit back and ignore the discussion, which is why I would usually select from each group in turn. Alternatively, I may say something like, 'This question is for those who support a football team who play in blue shirts, but when we have heard some answers, I will choose somebody from another group to comment on their answers, so be prepared.' (More on this as a technique later.) This will ensure that those who are in other groups will be forced to pay attention to this part of the discussion.

Selected groups can also be narrowed down, if required, by adding to the selection. For example, for the group who said they travelled to school in a car it is relatively easy to say, 'This question is only for those who travelled in a silver- or grey-coloured car.'

Using these random techniques not only gives a truer indication of learning across the group, but also ensures that students never know if they are going to be required to contribute next, meaning that even those not directly answering are forced to be more ready to take part – and this usually involves paying better attention to what other students are saying. This often has the added benefit of improving behaviour.

The combination of the three techniques mentioned so far should already improve the numbers of students taking part in the science discussion. However, there are also other techniques, many of which are especially useful with students who are reluctant to contribute verbally, or who are not actively listening to what other students are saying. The following techniques are particularly useful for students who want to 'opt out' of discussions, but they should not be seen as only being applicable to these students. All of these methods will help to encourage more active participation from more students in science discussions.

Making sure that students are actively listening

Having all the students involved in a discussion can rarely mean that every individual verbally contributes. What is essential, however, is that *every* student is ready to speak – on the edge of their seat – if called upon to do so. Questions such as those in the section above clearly mean that students have to be ready to not only provide knowledge and understanding in their answers, but also evidence of having been involved in the discussions, by *listening* to what everybody is saying. This is a very long way removed from the, unfortunately, all too typical science discussion that involves a lot of individual conversations between the teacher and a small number of individual students.

Clearly a change in behaviour and focus will help to indicate that students are involved in active listening, but there are a range of techniques that can be used to check this directly, which also help to promote active listening and greater involvement in discussions.

Asking the same question to several students

I would often start a discussion question by saying that I would listen to, for example, six answers to the question. I would then ask the question only once, e.g. 'What might happen if an animal evolved that could manufacture its own chlorophyll?' I would then listen to answers one after the other, from perhaps a whole subgroup (see page 72) or perhaps one student from each subgroup each time responding with a simple 'thank you' after each student's input. Even if two or three students had almost the same answer, I would still continue. However, often in this situation, what you will find is that students naturally build on answers that they have heard before, often referencing them, or they will search deeper within their own learning to add extra information. Alternatively, they may produce counter arguments to something they have heard. Many teachers will be surprised at how rarely students simply repeat exactly what a previous student has said, especially if the question – like the example above – is planned to allow for a wide range of potential answers.

One benefit of allowing several students to answer the same question, with nothing more than a 'thank you' in response, is that it obviously reduces the teacher's input to the discussion and increases student input, and therefore, more useful information is gained about *learning*.

An additional benefit of this approach is that it also avoids affecting the ego of students. All too often, when observing discussions in science lessons, I have seen the teacher ask a recall question to a group. If the first student answers incorrectly, they are usually told immediately that they are wrong, and this may happen to a few students – usually with more clues from the teacher each time – until eventually a student answers correctly, and is told that they are right. Think for a minute how this must make those students who answered incorrectly feel. Is this likely to make them volunteer an answer in future, especially if they are not 100% sure if their answer may be correct? It seems obvious to me that this approach is guaranteed to *narrow the number* of students prepared to take part, to the small group who were right. Allowing several answers, even if some are repetitive, shows students that their contribution is valued, and encourages further participation. It also gives a wider understanding of learning across the group.

Having listened to several answers, I would then select another random student to explain which answer they thought was best and why. Depending on the nature of the discussion, several students would also have been asked this same question: 'Who had the best answer and why?' In this way, from the starting position of one well-thought-out, high-level question, as many as a dozen students may have contributed ideas, showing a range of levels of understanding, or lack of it. All of them will have *actively listened* to what other students had to say. This,

I am sure you will agree, is a very long way from the typical science discussion that I described back at the start of this chapter.

Who said that?

Another simple technique for ensuring that students listen carefully to their peers is to ask one question that several students each answer, as in the example above, then to select another random student, and ask them which student used a particular word or phrase in their answer, e.g. 'Out of the six people, which one of them said atoms and molecules, instead of just using the word particles?' When I first tried this with a Year 7 class, I was met by bemused looks from the students, and 'I don't know' from a nervous girl. But within a couple of weeks, the students knew to expect this type of question, and they almost always spotted the word or phrase, and indeed saw it almost as a fun quiz challenge, with many students calling out, 'I know. I know.' This clearly demonstrated that their listening skills had improved.

I have used this technique, as with all of these techniques, across the age and ability range, *always* with great success.

X number of people have not yet answered

This works particularly well with larger, KS3 or lower sets of students. After having asked a couple of questions, where a large number of students have responded each time, I might then say, 'It's been great to hear from so many people. Only six people have not answered so far.' This would instantly get those who had not contributed an answer so far thinking that I had been specifically watching them. In turn, this would put more pressure on these individuals to respond to the next, or a later, question. You may often find some students will 'volunteer' their 'friends' at this stage, with a less-than-subtle, 'You haven't answered one yet, Olivia.'

Obviously, it helps to have a good idea of who has, and has not, answered – and often these will be the same students, lesson after lesson, particularly initially. However, even a general idea of the figure will be enough to persuade the students that you, as the teacher, have an 'all-seeing eye'. Interestingly, on at least two occasions when being observed by trainee teachers, they too have fallen for this, and have mentioned after the lesson how I seem to have a photographic memory for those who had not taken part in the discussion. One student even asked me how I was able to carry out the discussion and still know exactly which students had not contributed. She was shocked when I explained that I did not know exactly who all 'five' were, but that I was fairly sure that I had heard from most of the students.

Directly giving more thinking time

Higher-level questions such as, 'What might happen if global warming continues at the current rate?' or 'Why might some people worry about having vaccinations?' inevitably help to provide much greater information on the students' learning, in terms of knowledge, understanding, misconceptions, etc. than simple, low-level recall questions. However, to do higher-level questions justice, students need much *more* thinking time. Often, my first question – such as the ones above – would be asked before I took the register, giving the students a couple of minutes, rather than a few seconds, of thinking time. Following the register, I might then target a subgroup (see page 72) meaning that some other students would then get even more thinking time.

Another technique might be to tell the students exactly how much time they have to think about their answer. For example, 'You will be given exactly one minute to think of any answers to this question, after which I will select people, so don't bother calling out or putting your hands up before one minute is up.' One very important thing to note here is that if you do give the students a precise time like this, *never* extend it or shorten it. Use a clock and make sure it is precisely the time stated. I would often give a 15 or 10 second warning.

Some teachers may worry about the concentration or behaviour of some students if using this approach, and I am not going to say that this might not be a problem. What I would say is that coupled with other methods for encouraging participation in discussions, as already covered in this chapter, this technique will help to improve overall student participation. As with most of these techniques, it is not ideally meant as a stand-alone idea.

Think-Pair-Share

Another simple method of giving more thinking time is to give the students a short period of personal thinking time, perhaps 30 seconds or a minute, depending on the question. This personal time may, or may not, include the students being able to 'look back' at something in their science book or textbook. Students would then be given more time to talk about their ideas with a partner or perhaps in a small group; for example, two or three minutes. Finally, the question would be used as part of a whole-class discussion. By this point, many more students would be ready to be involved.

There is an added benefit of this technique in that the class discussion follows from pair or small group discussions, so individuals will inevitably start their responses with 'We thought...' rather than 'I thought...' Once more, this helps those students who might be less confident with their science ability or with giving verbal answers, as it removes any perceived 'blame' for any mistakes falling directly on them as individuals.

You will also generally find that the students will usually listen even more carefully to other responses, to see if anybody else was thinking along the same lines that they and their partner(s) were.

Keep quiet

As difficult as it can be, it is often much more beneficial if the teacher does not say anything, even if there is a pause. If a question is asked of an individual or a group and they do not respond fairly quickly, it is incredibly tempting to intervene with a clue or something else. If instead of doing this the teacher remains silent, more often than not, the student(s) will eventually say something. Even if the something is 'I have thought about it, but I really don't have a clue.' This in itself is useful information on *learning*, because at least that way the teacher knows that even with more thinking time, the particular student had not learned what was hoped for.

Many teachers will at this point be thinking, 'If I don't say anything, my students will just all start chatting.' To this I would say, firstly, you may be pleasantly surprised how long it is before anybody does interrupt. Secondly, as with the other techniques in this section, this is not a stand-alone idea. The more positive involvement by the students, either in contributing to, or actively listening to, the discussion by using the variety of these techniques, the more likely that a significantly longer period of silence than you might expect is likely to be successful. This is definitely a technique that teachers need to try to find out how it works.

CHAPTER 2: QUESTIONS AND DISCUSSIONS

You may be pleasantly surprised to find that particular groups gradually get better at keeping silent, for slightly longer. Different groups will undoubtedly be able to do so for different periods of time. The key point is to practise – both for the teacher and the students.

Phone a friend

To further encourage students to participate with discussions, try allowing each student the opportunity, on only one occasion during a lesson, to pass the question on to a classmate. Usually when I did this, I would insist that the classmate had to be somebody who had *not yet answered* a question. This does two things; firstly, it stops students always passing questions on to the same few peers, whom they see as 'best at science' in the group. And secondly, it again puts the emphasis on the student to know who has, and has not, already answered, which again reinforces active listening. Any student who was unable to identify a peer who had not yet answered, would not be allowed to pass the question on. You might be pleasantly surprised here to learn how often even those students who you think pay little attention are able to successfully identify another student who has not yet contributed. Once passed on to a friend, the question would then *have* to be answered by that student and could not be passed on again.

The other obvious benefit of this technique is that it means that students who have not yet taken part in the discussion also need to be actively listening and ready to offer a possible answer.

This technique can be adapted in a variety of ways. One method I used on occasion was to allow the student who was initially unable to answer to pass the question on to three different friends, after which the original student then had to explain which friend provided the best answer, and why they thought this.

However it is used, this technique definitely helps to keep students 'on the edge of their seat' during the discussion.

What to do with students who say, 'I don't know' or similar

One problem that I have often observed with discussions in science, is that teachers are often unaware of what to do if a student either does not want to answer or says something like, 'I don't know.' This is often where teachers resort to giving ever-more explicit clues to the individual, or simply moving on to another student who is prepared to answer, neither of which help to provide feedback on *learning* for the individual concerned.

My first advice for dealing with this is to make it clear to all classes early on, that not answering or saying 'I don't know' is *not* an option. I would remind students that in the same way they are not allowed to 'opt out' of other lesson tasks, they will not be allowed to do so with discussion work. Simply stating this as a fact will start to sow the seed in the students' minds that the discussions are of the *same* importance as the other lesson tasks. Obviously, simply stating this and not following through would be disastrous, so it is essential that the teacher then follows up on this, and insists that students participate fully.

I do realise, however, that on its own this may not be enough. At times I have had to insist with certain groups that instead of saying 'I don't know', students must instead select one of the following:

- 'Can I have some more time to think, please? Then when you come back to me I will definitely answer.'
- 'Can I ask a friend for some help with this, please?'
- 'Can I listen to two more answers before I give mine, please?

In all three of these cases it is important that the students realise that they can only use *one* of these, on *one* occasion, during a discussion/ lesson. This list might need to be put up on the board or a poster for some students to be able to remember them.

Secondly, it is vital that the teacher *does* go back to the student later during the discussion and *insists* that they contribute. In all three of these situations, students will have heard other responses before the teacher returns to hear from them. At the very least the students should then be encouraged to discuss what they have heard. Using prompts such as, 'Well, you have heard two other answers, which one did you prefer and why?' or 'Your friend said ... how might he/ she have improved his/her answer?' This technique not only allows students extra thinking time, but also forces them to *actively listen* to the responses of other students that, as mentioned earlier, is a key part of a successful discussion.

Finally, I am fully aware that there are those students who lack confidence or are, perhaps, just so bloody-minded, that they simply refuse to answer. For these instances, there are many additional techniques to get the students to be part of the discussion, without them feeling under so much pressure. The following techniques can all help to reduce pressure on an individual which, in turn, is likely to make them much more responsive.

Somebody else's mistake

Students who refuse to answer or give their thoughts often lack confidence, maybe generally or in their science ability. By making them talk about *other students'* answers, this shifts the emphasis from being 'me making mistakes, so I'm not going to do that' to 'well, it was he/she who said it, so if I get anything wrong it will be his/her fault.' This fundamentally changes the mindset of these individuals.

Questions such as:

- 'Could you add anything to what Sanjit said, please?'
- 'Can you explain what Amber meant by … please?'
- 'What do you think about what Caroline said about…?'
- 'What word or phrase might Mohammed have used instead of…?'
- 'How else might Sinita have described/explained…?'
- 'Do you agree with Mark? Why?'
- 'If there were X marks for that answer in the exam, how many do you think Shanice would get, and why?'
- 'I think what Oliver said would only get X marks. What else could you add to his answer to get Y marks?'
- 'What did Michaela say in her answer that might gain/lose marks in the exam?'
- 'Could you make a counter argument against Izzy please?'

All of these types of questions remove some of the initial fear that some students may have about 'being wrong', and also rely heavily on *actively listening* to what other students are saying during the discussion. The more often question stems like this are used, the more likely that all students in the group will be used to having to actively listen to the discussion, and the more prepared they are to contribute their thoughts, thus giving an insight into their learning.

Wrong answers are often most useful

As an AfL technique, clearly hearing students explain things incorrectly or make recall errors is extremely useful to a teacher, especially if, by using some of the techniques above, this has given a good indication of the scale of the misunderstanding in learning within the group. Incorrect answers should, wherever possible, be made use of, not ignored. For example, 'This answer had one small mistake in it, can anybody explain what it was?' In this way, not only will the teacher and students gain greater understanding of any misconceptions, but by showing that incorrect answers are just as useful as correct ones, the result will be that students are much less concerned about 'being right', and therefore much more willing to contribute to the discussion. This links back to the earlier idea on student ego. If providing a wrong answer is seen to be *useful*, then doing so is not such a negative ego hit.

Some teachers may be thinking that what I have just said is incorrect and that highlighting a student's answer as wrong would dent the student's ego. However, if this is a concern, there are ways of achieving the same result without appearing to be so negative – although hopefully you will have noticed that I said 'one *small* mistake' above, indicating that most of what was said was fine. An alternative way of wording to avoid such an obvious ego dent might be to say, 'How might an examiner have responded to that as a written answer?' This will not only allow other students to identify the error, but may also highlight the fact that others in the group are unaware that there was anything actually wrong with the answer. Clearly, this would work best if on some occasions you used the same question, even if the answer provided was perfect.

Again, if used in isolation this technique may not be hugely successful, but if coupled with many students responding to the same question, and students being used to the idea that some things they hear are 'better' and others 'not so good' but that all of the responses are *useful*, a culture develops where students are unafraid of providing answers that are 'wrong'.

Hands up

You may be surprised to see this as a subheading, as if you have followed the chapter so far, you would probably imagine that the type of discussion that I have advocated to provide useful feedback on learning would *not* involve students volunteering answers. Generally, this is correct, and usually I would not recommend students volunteering answers. Instead, the teacher should be using various selection techniques to decide who contributes. However, I worry that the 'no hands up' message may sometimes become too strict, and may, as a result, lead to failures in opportunities to encourage more students to be involved. Therefore, I would recommend using 'hands up' on occasion to boost overall student participation. This can be done in various ways.

A very simple use of 'hands up' might be to vote on two (or more) alternative answers. 'Which of the four answers we heard was best?' Votes like this do more than just encourage students to participate in the actual voting, but they encourage students to actively listen, especially if they are told in advance, for example, 'After listening to these four answers, we will all vote on which one best explains …' This is a great use of 'hands up'. Even more so if those who have voted for a particular answer are then randomly selected to justify their choice.

Another way to use 'hands up' is to get students to use it for *metacognition*. One way to do this might be – having reminded the students at the start of the discussion that they would need to use what they heard during it – to be able to write a sentence to show their understanding of the first learning objective. Part way through the discussion, the teacher could then say to the students, 'Put your hands up if you are already confident that you could write a sentence about the first learning objective.' Getting students to consider their confidence with something is always very useful, but will only really work if there is an atmosphere within class discussions where students are not afraid to be wrong, or to admit that they lack confidence. In my experience, it does not take many weeks with a new group to get to the stage where students are willing to not put their hands up in these situations, if the emphasis has been on discussions for learning, rather than simply ego boosting.

Another way of getting students involved in metacognition like this is to offer alternatives as to the level of confidence that students again vote on. I have often used fun ways of doing this, so I might say something like, 'Put your hand up if you can describe three key differences between elements and compounds, but only do so if you are confident enough that if you tried and got it wrong, I could give your best friend extra homework.' This always makes students laugh but, perhaps surprisingly, definitely encourages participation.

This would often be followed by me saying, 'Keep your hand up if you are confident enough with your understanding that if you got it wrong, I could give everybody on your table extra homework.' And then, 'Keep your hand up if you are still confident enough that if you were wrong, I could give everybody in the whole class extra homework.' These fun indicators would often provide really useful insight into the confidence in the learning of particularly tricky ideas.

After all of this, I would often select a student at random and rather than ask them to describe to me the three differences between elements and compounds, I would say something like, 'Please tell everybody why you are that confident.' This change in emphasis of the question would invariably lead to the explanation of the subject matter being given, or perhaps, with a less confident student, to a worry being expressed over a potential misunderstanding of this subject. In either case, because the student saw the question as being about their *confidence*, it removed the initial pressure of 'being right' about the subject matter.

The key point in all of these is that 'hands up' techniques can just as easily be used to encourage student participation, and to provide valuable feedback on learning to the teacher and the student as 'no hands up', if used creatively.

The student who is ultra-shy

There will be occasions when an individual student is extremely shy and seems totally unable to contribute verbally in front of the whole class. Forcing such students to be involved can be totally counterproductive, but this does not mean that these students do not need to be involved in the discussion.

At the early stages with such students, it is best to encourage them simply to take part in voting for other students' answers. In this way, they have to be active listeners and can still feel they are playing an active role. As time goes on, it might be that the student is asked to say if they agree or disagree with another answer, without any expectation of justification or, perhaps, to name which of several students he/she thought had the best answer, again with no expectation of justification. This low-level input is, however, still input and will encourage the student to realise that they still have a role to play in the discussion.

Encouraging extremely shy students to set themselves very small contribution targets with a self-reward system can also be productive, e.g. 'Aim to answer with one very short sentence in any one of the three lessons this week. If you do, treat yourself when you get home to your favourite food/chocolate.' The small targets can then gradually increase over time, so that the next target might be 'one small sentence in two of the three lessons this week.' Often extremely shy students feel that their shyness is 'fixed', whereas they fully understand that in all other things they do, such as learning to play an instrument, learning to drive, playing football, dance, etc. everything has to be mastered in small steps. However, rarely have I found that this same 'small steps' approach is either expected or taken with shyness. Yet, in my experience, these techniques can be *extremely* successful with the majority of very shy students.

Another way of dealing with the ultra-shy student is to allow them to contribute to you *privately* after the discussion. For example, after a discussion, you might ask them in a one-to-one situation which person they thought explained a particular topic best and why. The student would probably need forewarning of this, so that they were able to take special notice of the appropriate answers. Doing this again ensures that the shy student is, at the very least, an *active listener*.

Finally, with the ultra-shy student, I would encourage the science teacher to get the parents involved with the techniques you are using to encourage their son/daughter to take part during discussions. In my experience, parents are almost always both surprised by, and hugely supportive of, the 'small steps' and targets approach. Feedback from parents at parents' evenings has always been incredibly positive with this technique.

Finally – work on it

I know, both from my own experience and from that of other science teachers, that all the ideas and techniques in this chapter work perfectly well throughout the secondary school age, from Year 7 to Year 13, and across the whole spectrum of abilities, from those unable to read or write, to those gaining A* at A-level. However, as with all new ideas, it is essential *not* to expect instant success at the first time of trying. Different groups of students will respond differently to different techniques, picking up on some faster than others. From the teacher's perspective, however, it is vital to *persevere*, and not to expect students to change overnight. However, success will definitely come, and you too will have science discussions providing valuable information on *learning* to both teacher and students, and with the illusive 'edge-of-the-seat' atmosphere.

Chapter 3
Feedback

3:1 Introduction – why do I spend so much time marking work?

Without a doubt, marking work is the part of a teacher's life that every one of them could happily live without. If some form of artificial intelligence was invented that could mark students' work and provide feedback, it would surely be the most popular invention ever for those reading this book. However, at the same time, all teachers know that the interaction they have with students, both verbally and, even more so, when providing written feedback, is crucial to the progress in learning made by the students.

The very phrase 'marking work' is interesting. If you do an internet search of images of 'teacher marking work' you will almost certainly come across images like this:

Yet, if you change the search and look for images of 'teacher providing feedback' you will instead find images like this:

Clearly even the perception of 'marking' and 'feedback' at this simple level is very different, yet, interestingly, most teachers use the two terms interchangeably.

This chapter is about providing *feedback* to students. This may involve spending hours with piles of work or with electronic documents as shown in the first two images, but the key point is that to make the process worthwhile, the results should have the same effect on the students as the second set of images.

Finally, by way of introduction, I would like to reiterate that none of the ideas discussed in this chapter should in any way *add* to the workload of teachers. For most teachers, it is simply impossible to further extend the amount of time that they spend looking at students' work, so to suggest adding extra to this would obviously be pointless. Indeed, the key point of this chapter is how to provide meaningful feedback, in a smarter, more effective manner.

3:2 What is the purpose of feedback?

When you read this question, I would like to think that as a teacher, you would already have a very good idea of the answer. For most teachers, when considering this question, their thoughts are likely to include words such as: 'progress', 'improvement', 'correction', 'checking', etc. During the King's College Project, Dylan Wiliam described the purpose of feedback as follows:

> 'The main purpose of feedback is to improve the work of students on tasks they have not yet attempted.'

Stop here for a minute. Have a cup of coffee and a biscuit, and think about this statement. What are your thoughts on this summary of feedback? How does this statement make you feel? Is it even close to what you were thinking of as the purpose of marking? Dylan Wiliam went on to add more to his description of feedback, as follows:

> 'The important thing is not the feedback itself, but the student's reaction to the feedback.'

He has recently expanded on this idea to state that:

> 'The purpose of feedback is to improve the student, not the work.'

Stop again. Finish the coffee. Have another biscuit, and think about this statement. Is this how you see feedback? Look again at the earlier images associated with marking and feedback above. Does this statement fit with the images?

At this point, I do not intend to provide any more of an insight into the purpose of feedback. You may think, 'Well, why bother asking the question?' However, hopefully, both the images you have seen and Dylan Wiliam's comments have given you cause for reflection on why teachers provide feedback which, I think, is an ideal starting point to this chapter.

As probably the key feedback provided to students is in the form of written comments on their work, I will start by looking at some of the problems with, and methods of improving, written feedback.

3:3 Written feedback

The problems with written feedback

One of the easiest ways to see the problems with written feedback, especially in a subject like science, is to copy/photocopy teachers' written comments from students' books onto a separate piece of paper, and look at them in total isolation, without the student's work. Your first thoughts may well be that this is unfair, as the written comments are not isolated from the work. However, think on this: how often do students read the comments from their teachers, having first looked back through the work? Or are they more likely to simply read the comment on its own – in isolation?

Having carried this exercise out on many occasions with science teachers, it is not unusual to find written feedback with comments such as the following. These are all genuine examples, written by actual science teachers with a wide range of teaching experience, taken from one such exercise in a school rated by Ofsted as 'good':

- 'You need to put more details into your answers.'
- 'You have clearly understood most of today's work.'
- 'This homework has not been given enough time, care, or effort.'
- 'Poorly presented.'
- 'You can do much better than this.'
- 'Well done. A great effort, and very neatly presented too.'

Look again at these written comments. Give them a little thought. Perhaps have another biscuit.

Do you notice anything about these statements?

Many teachers' first reaction is to say that the comments are too brief, but is there anything else that you noticed? Have one last look at them, and the final biscuit – if there are any left.

How do you know these comments even came from *science* books? If the aim of these comments was to improve learning in *science*, or as Dylan Wiliam would say, 'To improve the student not the work', are these fit for purpose?

At this stage, in all likelihood, you may well be thinking to yourself that you write much longer, and more meaningful, comments on your students' work. However, an alternative problem that comes up during this exercise of 'looking at comments in isolation from the work', is that often teachers write far *too much* on student's work. They sometimes correct every single spelling error and write numerous sentences or even paragraphs of information at the end of the work, which all too often, when looked at in isolation, also provides very little clear guidance on *learning*. If you don't believe me, then I suggest you try this exercise out. I have done this with science teachers in a variety of schools, and almost without fail, they are always surprised with how little clear actual guidance their comments provide, whether short or long.

In both of these extremes, what is almost always missing is any link to *learning* – rather than completion of tasks – and any guidance on *how* to make improvements to learning.

Effective written feedback

Following on from the earlier comments by Dylan Wiliam on the purpose of feedback, one more point that Paul Black also made on the subject during the King's Project, was that he sees the most important aspect of written feedback as the fact that it should 'make the student think'. Again, just stop and think about this statement for a couple of minutes – after all, if you have already read chapter 2, you should know by now the importance of thinking time. (Although you may be out of biscuits by now.) Would you have considered 'making the students think' as at *all* important, when providing written feedback?

In keeping with the overall way in which AfL works, it would seem clear that when teachers provide written feedback, the comments should provide three basic pieces of information:

- Make clear to the student where they actually are in terms of the learning they *have* achieved
- Make clear to the student where they need to 'get to' in terms of their learning

and most importantly,

- Make clear to the student *how* to actually make this progress in their learning.

It is the last of these three points that I feel is so often missing from feedback – especially from written feedback, and particularly so in science.

Having read this, your first thoughts may well be that what is being asked for is going to be (a) difficult, and (b) will involve the teacher doing a lot more work. If done properly, however, neither of these should be the case. In fact, you may well be surprised to find out that not only is this remarkably easy to do, but that it will, in many cases, *reduce* the workload. Now when was the last time that somebody suggested something that would improve your teaching *and* reduce your work load?!

Using written feedback structures

The easiest way to ensure that written feedback tackles the three key AfL points above is to ensure that the feedback is very clearly organised, so that both the teacher and the student (and the parents, should they ever check the feedback) know precisely what the comments mean and where the three key points mentioned above actually are.

In turn, the simplest way of ensuring this is to have a precise *structure* to the written feedback. One very simple written feedback structure that has proven to be successful across all ages and abilities (and not just in science, but across all subjects) is as follows.

The first sentence of the feedback should clearly state if the *first learning* objective has or has not been achieved, with evidence if necessary, e.g.:

'Your answers to questions 1-3 show that you can describe what happens to the products of photosynthesis.'

Notice how in reading this statement, you should be able to see clearly what the first learning objective was, with no need to reread it. Thus, the comment can be read in isolation without the student needing to remind themselves of the first learning objective. The statement should also use as near to the exact wording of the first learning objective as possible, to reinforce this *learning language*.

The second sentence of the feedback should clearly state if the second learning objective has, or has not, been achieved, again with evidence if necessary, e.g.:

'Your answer to question 5 shows that you cannot explain why glucose has to be converted into starch for storage.'

Again, the *second learning objective* should be apparent from reading this statement. The student in this case is aware that they have failed to provide evidence of the learning objective and precisely what evidence was used to judge this. The student does not, therefore, need to reread all their work to identify their learning problems.

The third sentence (and fourth if one is required) should focus on precisely how improvements can be made, either in the short or long term, e.g.:

'You need to rewrite your answer to question 5 by considering the solubility of starch and sugar and how these might affect osmosis in the storage cells. If still unsure, ask me for help.'

Here, rather than vague suggestions, the student is provided with a precise description of exactly what is required in order to improve their learning, and even more importantly is provided with some additional guidance on *how* to actually make the improvement.

Three short sentences. Yet even when read in total isolation, these provide a clear indication to the student of precisely what the student can, and in this case, cannot do, and exactly *how* to make improvements. They also help to reinforce the language of learning that the initial work's learning objectives provided. All of this useful information on *learning*, in approximately 70 words!

In the third sentence on making improvements, it never ceases to amaze me how often teachers tell students that they need to improve something, without providing guidance on *how* to do so. I can remember having a similar discussion with a head of IT in a school who said that he was writing ever-longer feedback on what students needed to do to improve their work, but he found that, despite their high ability, they rarely took any notice of his feedback. I asked him to check to see if he used the word 'by' in his feedback. It turned out that he had not been doing so, and when later he did, he found student engagement vastly improved. This simple two-letter word is crucial to making guidance for improvement effective. It does, however, need to be followed by *precise* guidance as in the example above, not by vague phrases, such as, 'add more details', 'give this more thought', etc.

This is where having clear *success criteria* for learning for students is vital (see chapter 1). If the success criteria are clear, then it is easy to say if they have, or have not, been met. It should also be relatively easy to suggest simple, *precise* ways of making improvements to satisfy the criteria. Looking again at the example of the second and third sentences in the feedback above, it is immediately clear in the feedback that the teacher expected the learning objective on 'explaining why sugar is converted to starch' to be based on knowledge learned about the solubility of the two chemicals.

A simple structure of two 'what has/has not been achieved' statements, and a single 'how to make improvements' statement, should mean that in three, fairly straightforward sentences, *clear* and precise *feedback* related to learning can be provided.

Look for one last time at the three sentences given as examples above, and think again of the two purposes of feedback that Dylan Wiliam and Paul Black suggested earlier. Is this example of feedback fit for purpose?

This technique will, in many cases, *reduce* the time teachers take writing comments on students work, definitely for those who usually write several sentences when providing feedback. For those teachers who currently write only very short, ineffective comments, such as 'more details and effort required', although this technique may need them to write more than normal, they should at least appreciate that what they will be writing will be actually worthwhile, and actually will 'make their students think', rather than be a complete waste of the teacher's time. Surely it is better to write 70 useful words that improve *learning*, than half that number that achieve nothing.

This technique also builds naturally on a technique used in numerous primary schools, which many Year 7 students will already be used to, where their work may well have previously had feedback provided using **WWW – What Went Well** and **EBI – Even Better If...** statements.

Indeed, to encourage consistency of written feedback across the school (not just in science), I know that some schools have even used a stamp (these can be purchased online) that has the following on it, which staff use:

WWW1

WWW2

EBI

SR

SR in this case stands for **Student Response**, and is intended to provide space for the student to actually complete the task given to them in the **Even Better If...** part of the feedback. So, here would be where the student in the example above would rewrite their answer to question five, including more information about solubility of glucose and starch.

These types of stamps not only help to maintain a consistency of written feedback across a large number of staff, but they tend to be particularly useful and effective for less experienced teachers, and for younger or less able students. The stamp's format also limits the space available for the teacher to write, forcing teachers to be both more *concise*, and *precise*.

An alternative version of this type of 'assessment stamp' that has also been successfully adopted by some schools has the following prompts:

LO1

LO2

IB

SR

In this case **LO** clearly refers to the **Learning Objectives**, **IB** stands for **Improve By...** and **SR** for **Student Response**, as before.

Whether actual stamps or simply the prompt structure are used to provide guidelines, written feedback that follows a *regular structure* will not only prove to be far more effective in both engaging students in their learning, and giving students and parents greater *clarity*; it also has the added bonus of actually being – for many teachers – *quicker* to provide the written feedback. Gone are the evenings of trying to think of something to summarise thoughts on a whole piece of work. Gone too are all the 'filler' comments and student-ego related comments, such as, 'You can do better' or 'You have clearly put a lot of effort into this.'

What about written comments on effort and presentation?

You will notice with the feedback techniques above, there is no mention of either the student's effort or presentation. Clearly this does *not* mean that these are no longer of any importance. However, feedback should be centred on *learning*, and so if either effort or presentation are mentioned, they should be clearly *linked* to learning. Commenting on either of these as separate items, divorced from the student's learning, will at the very least downplay, and possibly overshadow, the key reasons for providing feedback. Imagine the student who spends time assuring that they properly meet the learning objectives for the work, only to be confronted by a statement complaining about their poor presentation. This is almost certain to 'make the student think', as Paul Black said was important, but are these thoughts likely to be productive to *learning*?

Linking written comments on presentation to learning

One way in which this can be done is by making one of the learning objectives about presentation. This would be used when presentation was actually something of particular importance in order to improve learning in an area of science. For example, when drawing graphs, students may be provided with a checklist of points on 'How to properly draw graphs' that would probably include advice such as, 'Use a ruler', 'Use more than half the paper', etc. This, by its nature, means that the *presentation* of the graph is important. Thus, one of the learning objectives might be something like 'To be able to use the rules on graphs to produce a graph on ...' In the same way, learning objectives could be linked to the presentation of tables, drawing of diagrams, etc. In these instances, what is important is that the students can clearly see that there is a *direct link* between the need for careful presentation and the progress in their *learning*.

The advantage of using presentation within a learning objective in this way is that students see the importance of presentation as a means of helping to improve their learning, rather than simply something to 'please their teacher' or to 'make their work look nice'. Linking presentation to learning like this is far more effective than simply 'nagging' students.

If presentation is not part of the learning objective for a whole class, it could still be mentioned in the 'Even better if...' or 'Improve by...' section of written feedback for particularly untidy students' work. The key here is to ensure that, as before, the idea of needing to improve presentation should be linked, once more, to *improving learning*.

Examples of this technique may look like this:

> 'Even better if you improve how easy it is to use your results table **by** repeating it, using a pencil and ruler, which will make it easier for you to see which figures are in which columns.'

> 'Improve your diagram **by** using a pencil and a ruler for all the straight lines, and enlarging it to at least half a page. This will make it easier for you to revise from in future.'

In both of these examples it is clear to the individual student that their presentation is 'sloppy', but more importantly, the comments highlight how this sloppiness can actually affect the student's progress in learning.

If, as a teacher, it is difficult to link the untidy presentation to improvements in learning, then the question should arise as to how important the 'scruffy' presentation actually is in terms of the student's progress. Not everybody writes/draws neatly, and while encouraging this is clearly important, it should never distract from the overall goal of *improving learning*.

If there really is a major problem with an individual student's presentation that is affecting the whole of their learning, or your ability as a teacher to assess that learning, then it may be necessary to examine whether the individual would benefit from some additional special educational support, or from using a computer to produce their work, etc.

Linking effort to learning

Commenting on a student's effort is always a difficult thing to do, particularly for home learning tasks. It is almost impossible to know the conditions under which an individual has completed a task done 'at home', and therefore the actual 'effort' that a student has had to put in to complete the work. Obviously, if the work is completed in class, under supervision, this becomes easier.

However, praising effort or challenging lack of effort as stand-alone written feedback, is counterproductive to the key point of *improving learning*. Almost without fail, praising effort will do little more than 'ego boost', while criticising effort will almost always bring a response from the student, such as, 'How does he/she know how hard I tried?' Both such comments are extremely unlikely to 'make students think' – certainly not in a positive way.

Praising effort is best done, as with praising presentation, by linking it to one of the learning objectives. This could be done as follows:

'You seem to have put extra effort into your description of the rock cycle, including all three rock types, using more examples than you usually do, and this has clearly helped your learning of this crucial work – well done.'

'Compared with when you last evaluated a graph of results, you seem to have put more time and effort into balancing your arguments on global warming this week – well done.'

In both of these cases, similar *language of learning* appears as that which the student would have encountered in their *learning* objectives, reinforcing the link between effort and actual progress in learning. This should always be the aim, to ensure that the student understands that their effort *directly* affected a particular aspect of their learning. Without doing this, effort will remain as a mysterious 'secondary force' removed from actual learning progress.

Criticising effort is best done through the 'Even better if...' or 'Improve by...' statements. Examples of this could be, for example:

> '**Even better if** you had put more effort into describing the differences between the three types of rock. Add to your descriptions **by** mentioning texture, colour and one other feature of each rock type.'

> 'Compared with your evaluation done last week, this one seems to lack time and effort. Why? **Improve** the evaluation **by** making sure you have **at least three** arguments for and against, then drawing your overall conclusion on global warming.'

In both of these instances, there is a similar language of learning used with the student's original learning objectives. There is also *precise* information on what else should have been done with the 'extra' effort. This is much more likely to *make the student think*, and reflect, on their effort than a vague statement simply criticising their overall effort.

Finally, but extremely importantly, when praising or criticising either presentation or effort, it is always much more productive if it is not only linked to the learning, but is *always* done in comparison with the students *own work*, rather than the work of other students. There is often nothing more disheartening, and more likely to be a barrier to learning progress, than for a student to feel that their presentation or effort is being compared to other students. Nor, in reality, does the work of other students actually make any difference whatsoever to the learning progress of an individual student. However, it is not uncommon to see statements such as, 'Everybody else used a ruler to draw the graph, why didn't you?' or 'Why are your descriptions of the rock cycle so much shorter than everybody else's?' These comments will indeed 'make the student think' but certainly not the sort of thoughts that would be in any way productive!

By comparing with their own previous standards, students will realise that they are not in competition with other students – a competition that many will feel they can never win – but in competition with *themselves* to continually improve their own standards, and as a result, their own *learning*. Far better to say something like, 'When you did the graph on forces in January, it was much neater, and easier to get the required information from than this one. Why? Now it will be harder to revise this graph than the last one.'

In conclusion *all* written feedback needs to focus on learning. It should be precise, concise, and informative. Using a language of learning with which the student is familiar through the relevant learning objectives should tell students *exactly how* to make progress. For the majority of teachers, doing this will not only be far more productive, but will fairly quickly turn out to take them *less time* than their regular practice. This has indeed been the case when these techniques have been adopted in a range of schools to date.

3:4 Verbal feedback

The problems with verbal feedback

It has already been mentioned in chapter 2 how teachers tend to dominate class discussions in science lessons, quite often by their need to feel that they have to give verbal feedback following every input made by a student. This is almost always counterproductive and not only slows the flow of discussions, making it harder for other students to follow ideas, but also makes it difficult for individual students to properly take on board the feedback. How to provide more effective verbal feedback during discussions has already been covered in chapter 2.

However, it is not only during discussion work where teachers give verbal feedback to individual students. This also happens when the teacher moves around the room during the lesson. However, here too, there are often problems with the feedback.

One of the main problems with one-to-one feedback, as the science teacher moves around the room, is similar to those with written feedback; too often the comments are about effort, which is almost always in comparison to the effort of other students. The exact same principles apply here as with written feedback on effort mentioned above. Basically, the majority of these comments tend to be either ego boosters or 'ego bashers'.

However, by far the biggest problem with verbal feedback is that it very rarely mentions *learning*, or the learning objectives. If not talking about effort, concentration, behaviour, etc. at best, comments tend to focus on *tasks*, as separate from the actual learning. 'You need to stop chatting, get the table of results finished, and get on to the graph. Everybody else is already doing the graph.' This would be a fairly typical piece of verbal feedback during a science lesson. (Admit it, you recognise comments exactly like this.) As a piece of feedback, this would certainly *cause a reaction* from the student which is, after all, what Dylan Wiliam said feedback should do. However, I am unsure if the reaction would always be a positive one, or one that would improve progress in learning. Feedback like this will undoubtedly 'make the student think', as Paul Black said was very important, but again, I am fairly certain that any thoughts going through the student's mind regarding the feedback are likely not to be particularly pleasant ones!

Effective verbal feedback

As with written feedback, what is being suggested here is *not* to ignore comments on behaviour, effort, concentration, etc. but instead to link these to *learning*, and more precisely, if possible, to the completion of learning objectives. In this way, students will see the *process of learning* and the learning objectives as central to the lesson, rather than behaving and concentrating as being the key factors. Indeed, when observing science lessons, it has often occurred to me that by the number of times either 'behaviour' or 'concentration' are mentioned, these are often seen as the key objectives by the teacher, and presumably, therefore, by the students.

I am fully aware at this point that there will be teachers reading this who will be screaming out things like, 'Unless they behave, or concentrate, they won't learn anything' and 'Am I supposed to just let them behave how they like?' Obviously, I am not advocating student anarchy, nor could I agree more that unless students behave and concentrate well, they will not learn as well as possible. However, it is important that both the teacher and the student realise that improved behaviour is a means to an end – the improvement of learning – rather than an end in itself.

Let's start by looking at the more positive type of verbal feedback, before going on, later, to look at more critical verbal feedback.

Praising effort and behaviour verbally

This should always be done individually wherever possible, although it could easily be linked to a small group of students. However, the praise should be *precisely* linked to the idea of progress in learning – *not* to the *completion of tasks*. Otherwise students will see task completion, rather than success in learning, as their key goal, and these are rarely the same.

Examples of ways to link praise to learning could be as follows:

- 'Well done Jenny, you seem to be concentrating well today, and it looks like you have already got enough ideas down to show that you can describe the four main forces at work on a floating object.'
- 'Well done Kathy, you seem to be using all the key scientific words to explain the process of combustion.'
- 'Well done, Mandeep. I can see that you have already started work on the second learning objective, which is excellent, as you have only been working on it for fifteen minutes.'
- 'Peter, you seem to be making quicker process through the learning objectives today than usual. I wonder if that is because you are chatting less today than normal? Well done.'

By referring *directly* to the actual phrasing of the learning objectives or by using the words 'learning' or 'learning objectives' in this type of feedback, in the minds of the students it switches the feedback from being ego-driven to being about *progress in learning*. Look again at the first two of these examples; can you tell what the learning objective was for the work?

Posing the question about the link between improved learning and improved behaviour, as in the final example above, is a good way to get the student to self-reflect on their improved learning. In this case, Peter may or may not consider that he has been chatting less than normal, but either way, he will almost certainly consider the effect of his chatting on the *progress* of his learning.

Criticising effort and behaviour verbally

This is even more essential to do individually wherever possible, but again, it could be aimed at a very small group of students – *never* a whole class. The key thing is *not* to compare the students with others in the group but to make comparisons, if necessary, with the same students previously and to link all comments directly to the negative impact on *learning*.

If students' effort and behaviour are compared with others in the group, some will always see this as an 'unfair competition' – one which they could never win. 'How could I ever be as good as him/her?' Or there are those who will feel that if they are unable to come 'top' in this 'competition', then they will stand out by being 'bottom'. 'I haven't even finished the first question yet. Ha ha.' Or, as they say in the wonderful *Bugsy Malone* musical, 'I'm the very best at being bad!'

To avoid these situations, the following are examples of verbal comments that could criticise effort or behaviour by directly linking the effort/behaviour – *not the child* – to learning.

> 'Desdemona, you seem to have completed less work in 15 minutes than you normally do. Do you need help with describing the process of convection? Can you remember the three key scientific words you needed to include?'

This comment, while criticising the amount of work done, does *not* compare Desdemona to other students, and helps to refocus her mind on what needs to be done to achieve the first learning objective in terms of success criteria. (Can you spot what the learning objective is, when you reread this comment?) This in turn links the lack of work to the lack of success in this first learning objective.

> 'Ikram, you have spent so much time chatting that you have only given one example of why friction is important for a car. You needed "at least three" for the first learning objective. You heard at least five examples in the discussion earlier. I will give you three minutes only to add two more examples.'

While making it clear that Ikram has not completed enough work, this comment again reminds him what *progress in learning* looks like, and also provides a clue as to *how* to complete this progress.

'Francesca, you have only balanced two of the equations so far. They show that you can do them, and the next three should be of similar difficulty. If you are unsure, do them in pencil, but you need to complete five examples to show you have done the second learning objective. How quickly do you think you will be able to do them?'

This comment again focuses on *exactly* what is required to demonstrate learning, but rather than focus the criticism on the lack of effort, it gives the student two options. Firstly, it considers that perhaps Francesca may be struggling but that she is too embarrassed to ask for help. By raising this as a possibility, this gives Francesca an easy way to admit she is finding the task difficult.

The suggestion of her using a pencil (with the option of correcting later) considers the fact that Francesca may not require help but may simply be lacking confidence with the task.

Finally, by asking her to consider how quickly she might be able to complete the learning, this forces Francesca into considering which of these first two options is correct. Clearly, if she is simply lacking confidence, the task should not take as long to complete than if she requires help. Actually requiring an answer to the question of how long it may take her to complete the task, rather than asking it rhetorically, would force Francesca to consider if it is simply her behaviour, and not any problems with the work that have caused her to be behind.

You will notice that all three of these examples are slightly longer than perhaps written feedback comments are. Again, you may be thinking, 'How will I have time to say all this to every student?' However, by using more precise verbal feedback linked to learning, you will usually find that there is much less need to repeat feedback to the same students, which happens more often with vague verbal feedback such as, 'Stop talking and get on.' (Admit it, this is another one you recognise only too well.)

Finally, criticism of *presentation* is often done verbally during one-to-one discussions, but as with written work, this should always be linked to progress in learning – see chapter 2.

One way of doing this, for example, might be to say something like this:

'Kieran, your table of results is very messy. You might be able to understand it now, but without any units or proper headings, you will find it almost impossible to complete the graph you need for the second learning objective. I guarantee you that five minutes improving the table now will save you 10 minutes later when doing the graph. So, you will end up doing five minutes less work – bonus!'

This comment not only links the presentation to progress in learning, but also suggests a possible motive for the untidy table, without *directly* calling Kieran 'lazy', etc. By suggesting that the end result will be 'less work' it also makes Kieran see that the *learning progress*, rather than the amount of work/effort/time, is the most important part of the lesson.

As you can – hopefully – see, the key thing about these types of feedback is that they concentrate on progress in learning. They also help to reinforce the learning objectives during the lesson, in subtle but important ways, making these learning objectives the focus of the *whole lesson*, rather than only at the start and the end. Finally, these techniques use this same *language of learning* during the lesson as the students will, hopefully, see later in their written feedback, highlighting the key aspect of this approach to using AfL, in that it is an all-encompassing way of teaching, rather than just something added to lessons.

Verbal feedback during discussions

As was mentioned during chapter 2, teachers too often dominate class discussions during science lessons. Often this can be by continually providing verbal feedback to every student who contributes. Thus the 'class' discussion actually becomes a repeated set of 'teacher-student-teacher' interactions. This is probably one of the more difficult habits for teachers to change when adopting a more *learning-centred* approach to their teaching. However, with use of a few techniques, the verbal feedback during discussions can be cut considerably, allowing far greater input by (more) students.

Techniques to cut verbal feedback during discussions
The number of answers is a very simple technique that will dramatically reduce the teacher input that was described earlier in chapter 2, but is worth repeating here. It involves stating *before asking*

a question of the group how many (perhaps a minimum) students the teacher will hear speak before they next intervene. For example, 'I am going to listen to at least six people's opinions on what might happen to food chains if some animals could do photosynthesis. I am not going to comment on them at all during this stage.' The teacher would then select six or more students to provide answers, and after each one, simply say 'Thank you' before moving on.

After the students have all been heard, the teacher could, if they feel necessary, provide general feedback on the comments, such as, 'All the people who answered clearly understand the importance of photosynthesis at the start of food chains. Well done to all of those who took part' or 'Well, you have now heard enough different, but very useful, ideas to come up with at least three ideas of your own, which I would like you to use to answer the next written question.' In both of these cases, general feedback is provided for the six students who answered, which is just as effective, and meaningful, as saying 'Thank you' to the individuals.

As mentioned in chapter 2, an alternative type of verbal feedback during group discussions might be to then select some other students to summarise what they thought were the 'best' ideas, and why. This gets even more students involved, and means that the verbal feedback is actually being provided by other students, rather than by the teacher, which is often more powerful.

Another method of feedback that works well with even larger numbers of students answering is to give general feedback, such as, 'Well, I would say that 10 of those 12 answers show that people can clearly describe the importance of plants at the start of food chains.' This statement helps to reinforce a learning objective, but also links back to Paul Black's point that 'feedback should make students think'. Undoubtedly, not only the 12 students involved but also the others who listened would immediately be thinking about which two of the answers did not reflect this learning, and which did. Leaving this for the students to decide, rather than actually telling them, is again a very powerful learning tool.

A particular benefit of these methods of group verbal feedback is that the students who do take part will also realise that their contribution is being measured not by the effort, nor if it is 'right or wrong', but simply if it helps with the progress of the learning towards a particular objective. This will *undoubtedly* encourage more students to participate in the discussion.

Encouraging self-reflection is another technique that can dramatically reduce the verbal feedback provided by a teacher during a class discussion. Again, this should be flagged up to the students at the *start* of the discussion. For example, 'We are going to have a discussion to see if you can use the information you read on neutralisation to describe why the process is important in everyday life. After the discussion, I want you to consider how well your answers compared to the answers of other students.'

After listening to as many different responses from different students as possible, you could ask the students to take part in a simple thumbs up/down – for better/worse – process to indicate how they felt their responses/understanding compared with other responses that they heard. This could even be done as a 'blind' exercise, where students close their eyes before giving their feedback. Alternatively, it could be done as a simple written exercise, as part of the lesson plenary, where students are asked to explain how their feedback compared with others they heard, and why they thought this.

As before, this gets more students involved in the discussion with *less* verbal feedback from the teacher, and the emphasis on student responses being linked to *learning*, rather than effort.

Private feedback. Another technique that reduces the verbal feedback of a teacher during class discussions is to keep individual feedback until later in the lesson, when students are working on other tasks. In this way, a few individuals could be targeted with positive or negative verbal feedback, similar to those mentioned on pages 103 and 104, about their contributions to the discussion, e.g. 'Well done, Vicky, it was nice to hear you give some good reasons for ... to the discussion earlier. It shows you have learned what is needed for the second learning objective.'

A quick, private word like this is not only much preferred by most students, but also makes the individual realise that (a) you were actively listening to their actual answers, and (b) that you thought so much of their contribution that you remembered it and mentioned it later. As such, this type of verbal feedback is extremely powerful.

Negative verbal feedback can also be done personally using this approach, e.g. 'You didn't have any ideas to share during the discussion on ... earlier, Mandeep. Do you need any help with describing ... or are you OK with doing this now that you have listened to other people's ideas?'

This is also very powerful as individual feedback, as not only does it make the student realise that you noticed their lack of learning – notice it is *not* the student's 'effort' or contribution that was criticised – this type of feedback also makes the assumption that the student, although possibly lacking in their own knowledge, *was* listening to other students, and reinforces the fact that doing this improves learning. Finally, by asking if the student needs any further help with the learning, the teacher makes it clear that it is *progress in learning*, rather than the student actually contributing verbally to the discussion, that the teacher sees as ultimately most important.

Summary

With both written and verbal feedback, it is important that the focus is *always* on progress in learning. Students should be constantly seeing and hearing the *same type of phrases* at the start of the lesson, in their learning objectives, during the introduction of discussions, in verbal feedback that they receive during the lesson, and then, finally, as written feedback when their work is assessed. This use of similar *learning language* that continually reinforces what is/is not required for progress in learning will quickly become second nature to both the teacher *and the students*, and is the key to high-quality written and verbal feedback.

Chapter 4
Peer and self-assessment

4:1 Introduction – the importance of peer and self-assessment

Way back in 2008, when Ofsted published *Assessment for Learning: The Impact of National Strategy Support*, it contained the following statement: 'The drawing together of learning during lessons and opportunities for pupils to assess their own work and that of their peers, were still rare ... However, they were key features to the most successful lessons.'[8] This was a reflection on findings across the range of secondary school subjects. Unfortunately, particularly in science, this statement still holds true today. Peer and self-assessment are still rarely done, and unfortunately, even when they are done, they are all too rarely done well. But why is this? Why is it that skills that most students have used very effectively in primary schools seem to cause such problems in science lessons?

---

8   Ofsted. (2008) *Assessment for learning: the impact of National Strategy support*. London: Ofsted.

4:2 What are the problems with students' peer and self-assessment?

Probably the major problem is the fact that unfortunately, for many science teachers, their own assessment is not often actually focused on *progress in learning*. I would like to suggest at this stage that if you have not already read chapter 3 on feedback, it would be wise to do so before going any further through this section, as the rest of this chapter assumes that you have done so.

Most schools nowadays have some sort of 'assessment/marking scrutiny', where teachers have their written feedback to students 'checked' by senior staff. I have yet to work in, or visit, a school where such 'assessment checks' have proven that 100% of the staff are doing written assessment 'very well'. On the contrary, usually a number of staff are identified who are struggling to meet the demands for high-quality written feedback. These may be less experienced teachers, but that is not always the case. On many occasions, teachers with years of experience are still seen to be struggling to provide high-quality written feedback. Using this information as a starting point, surely the question of why students are poor at peer and self-assessment should be turned around, to become 'Why should we expect untrained teenagers to be able to assess work and provide feedback on it, when trained, sometimes experienced, teachers are unable to do so?' Instead of bemoaning the fact that most students are not very good at peer or self-assessment, should we not be astounded that even *some* of our students are able to do so?

If science teachers are asked to explain the problems with their students doing peer or self-assessment, which I have done on many occasions, usually the following points tend to come up, in no particular order of importance:

- Students are more concerned about not upsetting their friends than in providing useful feedback.
- Students tend to judge other students depending on their personalities, rather than on the work itself.
- Students tend to emphasise effort and presentation rather than the actual work, concentrating more on the neatness, 'look', etc.

- Students are unable to actually write what they want to say about the work, through lack of the necessary language skills.

- Students in their teenage years tend to say that everything is 'OK', never wishing to commit to anything away from the 'norm', in order to have a 'quiet life'.

- Students rarely mention *learning* in their feedback.

This list is far from exhaustive, but summarises the type of problems that science teachers have when trying to involve their students in assessment. Coupled with the pressures of time that science teachers invariably find themselves under, it is not surprising that so many simply give up, and view peer and self-assessment as a lost cause.

Another problem that I have often encountered with peer and self-assessment in science lessons, is that teachers say they are doing this, when actually what they are doing is peer or self-*marking* – swapping books and marking another student's work. This is *not* peer (or self) assessment. I will refer you back to chapter 3 on feedback if you are unsure of the difference between marking and assessment, but the same rules apply here. *Assessing* work is all about providing **feedback on learning**, not simply allocating marks.

To totally embrace Assessment for Learning, however, it is worth remembering that peer and self-assessment is an integral part of the AfL jigsaw, which was recognised many years ago in the King's College *Working Inside the Black Box* publication. As such, it simply cannot just be 'pushed aside' and ignored. As with other aspects of AfL, it simply needs alternative strategies in order to ensure success.

4:3 How to get students to do high-quality peer assessment

One thing I hope you may have noticed so far in this chapter, is that the phrase 'peer and self-assessment' has replaced the more 'normal' version, which usually mentions 'self and peer assessment'. There is a very good reason for this, and it is not just me being pedantic or awkward. Students usually find self-assessment a much harder skill than peer assessment, so it makes sense to get your students used to doing peer assessment *before* they move on to self-assessment. Too many teachers will attempt to do these in the opposite order or both at the same time. From my experience I would strongly recommend that you *always* start with students doing peer assessment, and mastering that at a particular level, before introducing self-assessment.

As with all other aspects of learning, students will need to be 'trained' in doing peer assessment. They will need to be introduced to the simplest methods of assessing somebody else's learning, and to gradually improve this skill, until they are eventually able to complete the task on their own. Expecting students to be able to 'jump straight in' at the end of this journey, and to totally master peer assessment, seems to me no more logical than expecting a student to take on A-level work when they are only in Year 7.

What follows now is a simple structure for training students in the skill of peer assessment.

Starting out with peer assessment

For the lowest ages or attainment levels of students, I would suggest starting peer assessment by providing almost complete sentences with simple gaps for the students to fill in. For example:

> 'You have/have not (cross out as required) been able to describe at least three differences between metals and non-metals, because you mentioned _____ _____ and _____ .'

Or

> 'You have/have not (cross out as required) been able to describe the reactivity series of metals, because you were able to say that _____ and _____ were more reactive than _____ and _____ .'

What is – hopefully – obvious from these two examples is what the corresponding *learning objectives* from the lesson would have been. Did you spot them? This is yet another continuation of the *language of learning* that the students should be becoming familiar with, if you have read the earlier chapters.

Using almost complete sentences like this, focusing on the type of written feedback mentioned in chapter 3, will instantly avoid the whole list of 'problems' with peer assessment on pages 112-113 . As a teacher, you may feel that you are doing most of the work on peer assessment at this stage, but look again at what the students are actually doing. They are using their *own* judgement to decide what *evidence* there is for a particular learning objective being met. In other words, they are providing feedback on learning.

It is important at this stage to ensure that the students do *not* add any of their own comments. Otherwise, they will tend to write ego-boosting comments, such as 'well done', 'neat work', or perhaps even 'silly' comments to impress their friends, such as 'loser', etc. It is *vital* that from this very first stage, the students realise that they are only writing about **learning progress**, and nothing else.

Alongside the comments that the students complete on learning progress should also be some **peer advice**. Again, at the simplest level, this needs to be completely structured in advance, so that the students can concentrate fully on their decisions. For example:

> 'You only described _____ (insert number) adaptations of a plant living in a desert. You could improve this **by** adding _____ (insert number) more, such as by describing _____ , to show you have fully learned this.'

Or

> 'Your pH scale would be better **by** adding _____ (insert number) more examples of chemicals to pH numbers _____ .'

These examples also reinforce the idea that providing guidance on learning progress needs to include the word 'by'.

These two skills of commenting on learning progress and providing peer advice are *separate* skills, and could even be practised separately by students, until they are confident with completing them using these structured frameworks.

Moving on with peer assessment

Once a teacher is happy that the students have mastered the basic level of providing peer assessment on **progress in learning** and **peer guidance**, then the next stage is to allow the students to move away from filling gaps in sentences and towards completing sentences. For example:

'You have/have not described what happens when metals react with acids, and I can tell this because...'

Or

'You have/have not been able to describe how a convection current heats a room, and I can tell this because...'

Once more, it should be abundantly clear what the learning objectives were for each of these pieces of work. At this level, the students are given more freedom in selecting what *evidence* they use to suggest that a learning objective has, or has not, been met.

In the same way, providing *peer guidance* at this level would also involve students being provided with the start of a sentence, which they complete using as much evidence as they feel is necessary. For example:

'Your descriptions of the impact of global warming on the environment could be made better **by** adding...'

Or

'Your comparison of the difference between current in series and parallel circuits could be made better **by**...'

As before, it is essential to ensure that students only comment on the learning progress or guidance, and do not add additional comments about presentation, effort, etc.

Mastering peer assessment

Once the students are able to comfortably complete starter sentences for peer assessment on learning progress or peer guidance, then the final stage in mastering peer assessment would be to simply state what the assessment needs to include. For example:

'The first sentence must be about the first learning objective, saying what *evidence* that you can find to justify saying that the work reflects this learning.'

Or

'The second sentence must be about the second learning objective, and will need to provide the *best piece of evidence* you can find to demonstrate this learning.'

By the time students are working at this level of providing peer assessment on learning progress, they should be able to complete peer guidance in a similar manner. For example:

'Your "Even Better If..." sentence needs to say what other examples they could add to their work to better show they can explain how fossil fuels cause global warming.'

Or

'Your "Improve by..." sentence needs to say whether they missed out or misused any key words needed to explain how the lower arm is raised and lowered.'

Even at this level, hopefully, the learning objectives from the lessons are still clear in what the students are being asked to do during their peer assessment. Maintaining this clear *language of learning*, in all aspects of the students work, will continually reinforce progress in learning.

Peer assessing presentation

As with teachers providing written feedback – see chapter 3 – there may be times when you want your students to comment on presentation as part of their peer assessment. The most important thing about this, however, is that any of their comments *must* be linked to *learning*.

At a simple level, an almost complete sentence could be provided as guidance for students to complete. For example:

'You have described how friction occurs using diagrams, and your presentation *helped/hindered your learning* because...'

As always, the learning objective should be clear from this sentence. You should notice that this is similar to the intermediate level of providing peer assessment on learning or peer guidance.

This skill can be developed by making the students think not only about the presentation as it appears now, but how it may be of value *in the future* for learning. For example:

'You have explained what happens to each of the products of photosynthesis, and this will/will not be easy to learn when you revise because your presentation...'

Eventually, this skill should be able to be completed using guidance sentences. For example:

> 'In your "Even better if..." comment, suggest how their presentation could be improved to make their revision of the first learning objective even easier.'

This focus on *learning*, *evidence* and *specific guidance* will enable *all* students to provide useful peer assessment, even if some may never be able to move beyond the initial stage simply because of their language skills. Indeed, for some students with particularly low language skills, the peer assessment may even be given verbally, which I have found to be equally successful.

Looking again at pages 112-113 at the list of problems with peer assessment, it should be clear that providing a structure for peer assessment, at whatever level, should ensure success and eliminate all of the problems. Like all skills, however, these will need to be continually practised and developed. If students provided with the very first stage of guidance rarely ever practise it, do *not* expect them to move on to higher levels simply because they are older.

To not use any of these peer assessment structures, and to simply hope that students will be able to peer assess work because they are a certain age or of a certain ability, makes absolutely no sense. This would be like expecting a 25-year-old university graduate to instantly be able to drive a car, having never had any lessons, simply based on their age and intelligence. Obviously, nobody would expect this, so why expect students to be able to peer assess based on anything other than the level at which they have developed this skill?

4:4 How to get students to do high-quality self-assessment

Why is self-assessment difficult?

As mentioned earlier, self-assessment is usually much harder for most students to master than peer assessment, so it makes sense to only work on this after a certain level of competency at peer assessment is achieved. It is difficult to say exactly what level of mastery of peer assessment will be required, as this will very much depend on the students and their previous experiences of self-assessment.

The problems with self-assessment generally arise from the personalities of students. There are those students who are overconfident, who will always think that everything they do is amazing. Alternatively, there are the opposite students, those who lack self-confidence and will always underestimate themselves, and by reflection, their work. Finally, there is the problem all too familiar to any parent of teenage children. When asked 'How was your day at school?' (a seemingly simple piece of self-assessment), most teenagers will almost invariably answer with 'OK'. This will inevitably translate to any self-assessment tasks by 'playing it safe' – neither highlighting things that went well, nor those parts that did not go so well, and instead opting for 'a quiet life'.

To overcome these problems, as with peer assessment, simple structures are required that prevent the student from falling back on their 'easy option' responses.

Starting out with self-assessment

The first stage of self-assessment roughly corresponds to the second stage of peer assessment, as described on pages 115-116. At this 'starter' stage, the best way to get students to self-assess is to ask them to respond to the teacher's (preferably) written feedback or possibly to some peer assessment. For example:

'I agree/disagree with your/their comment on the first learning objective because...'

Clearly, this will only be successful if the teacher's written feedback that they are reflecting on is of high quality – see chapter 3 – as with peer assessment work (see earlier in this chapter).

By asking students to comment on the *feedback* rather than directly on their own learning – assuming that the feedback is of high quality – then whether they agree or disagree is irrelevant. What is important is that the comment they are referring to should not be about effort or presentation, but *progress in learning* – highlighted in this example, by referring directly to the learning objective. As such, in order to respond to the feedback that they have been provided with, the student will be compelled to consider their own progress in learning. Even if a student in their first attempt at responding in this way said something like, 'I disagree, because I put a lot of effort in' or 'I disagree because it was much neater than normal' it would be relatively easy to point out to the student that they had not addressed the task, which was about *progress of learning*, and they should be justifying their comment in terms of the first learning objective.

Other starter sentences for simple self-assessment might be:

> 'I agree/disagree that I can explain refraction using a diagram because...'

Or

> 'I agree/disagree that I can describe at least three differences between group 1 and group 2 metals because...'

As always, it should be fairly easy for you to spot in these what the original lesson's learning objectives were, maintaining the consistent language of learning.

Rather than respond to written feedback on *achievement*, the student could be encouraged to respond to the written feedback that provided them with *guidance* for improvement in a similar manner. For example:

> 'I agree/disagree with your/their suggestions for improving my work by ... because...'

Again, here the student is forced into narrowing their response to fit precisely with the guidance they were given on improving their learning.

These starter sentences and any others that follow the same type of pattern will remove the problems listed above with self-assessment, as they severely restrict what the student is able to actually write and force the student to *justify* any comments they make.

It would be wise to ensure that students are totally confident with doing both of these types of basic self-assessment before moving on any further.

Moving on with self-assessment

As students feel more confident with responding to your (or peer) written feedback, they should be able to use similar responses to start to do their own self-assessment of their learning progress. These will, as always, need guidance. For example:

'I think I have described how friction occurs between two surfaces because I have...'

Or

'I think I have explained where copper belongs in the reactivity series of metals because I have...'

Again, the starter sentence should follow directly on from the learning objective, which should be the *sole focus* of the self-assessment. (Hopefully, as always, the learning objective for the work is clear in these examples.)

As the students progress and become more confident with self-assessment at this stage, they could start to simply use the learning objectives and search for evidence to justify their own learning progress. A simple structure for this stage may be:

'How much evidence do you have in your work to show that you have completed the first learning objective?'

Or

'How many differences between the properties of metals and non-metals did you use in your work?'

A probe such as this will allow students to respond at a variety of levels, from a simple statement of facts to more detailed explanation of their evidence. The key point is that once more the student is simply focusing on the *progress in their learning*.

In the same way, simple self-guidance for improvement can be encouraged using restrictive starter sentences. For example:

'My comparison of the properties of the three types of radiation would have been better if I had...'

Here too, the focus is on the student looking for *evidence* of a precise piece of learning, and commenting on that evidence. I am sure you will agree that this is a long way removed from simply asking or expecting students to comment freely on 'how well they think they have done today'.

Mastering self-assessment

At the highest level of self-assessment, the student should be involved in **metacognition** – not only reflecting on what they have learned, but also considering the actual *learning process* itself.

This would be most appropriate not only for students who have already mastered the previous levels of self-assessment, but also when the learning objectives themselves are of a higher level. For example:

> 'The second learning objective asked you to evaluate your conclusions. Highlight each piece of evidence in your work that shows you have completed this objective. State how many pieces of evidence you found and *why* you think this is enough evidence.'

In this example the student may respond by discussing the actual number of pieces of evidence, where a larger number may be used to signify having achieved the learning objective, or they may instead comment on the fact that although the number of pieces of evidence may be 'low', the quality of their arguments for each was high, and that this provides evidence of having achieved the learning objective. In either case, the student is by now self-assessing the progress in their learning in a much deeper manner.

An alternative starting point for self-assessment at this highest level, might be as follows:

> 'What are the *best* two pieces of evidence you have that show that you met the first learning objective? Say *why* you think these are best.'

Here again, the student is forced to self-assess their work, not just in terms of if it provides evidence of progress in learning, but also to consider how *suitable* that evidence actually is.

At the highest levels of self-assessment, encouraging students to reflect on self-guidance requires students to look beyond simple points for improvement, and to consider how their work might be improved more *holistically*. One method for encouraging this is as follows:

> 'If you had an extra 15 minutes to explain how useful anaerobic reaction is in humans, what else would you add to your work, *and why*?'

This example, once more, encourages students to self-assess improvements to their work in a very different way. Does the work suffer from lack of content, lack of detailed explanation, lack of scientific terminology, poor presentation and so on? Which of these might have improved their work?

An alternative way of getting students to self-assess how to improve their learning, at the highest level, might be as follows:

> 'If you wanted to demonstrate an even *higher* level of learning for the second learning objective, which *one* of your points might you have developed further, and why?'

This limits the student to considering only one aspect of their learning, but again opens up the same list of possible ways in which the student may consider that this chosen aspect may be improved upon.

If you compare the three levels of developing peer assessment with the three levels for developing self-assessment discussed earlier, hopefully it is clear that these are two quite separate skills for students to master, which will *each* have to be developed at their own pace. Each of these skills will need to be *continually* practised in order to ensure that the students develop their best habits. Neither teachers, nor students, should ever feel able to say that they have 'done' peer or self-assessment, as if either of them can simply be mastered at a single stroke. Instead, both teacher and students should see these as two separate skills that can be continually improved, alongside all other aspects of learning in science.

And finally, on self-assessment...

Once students are confident with self-assessment, a fantastic plenary exercise that involves students self-assessing their learning in an interesting and unusual way, is to use the following idea as a lesson plenary:

> 'If you could go forward in time until just before you were going to answer an exam question on today's work, what two pieces of advice would you give yourself and why?'

This is a great plenary – probably my all-time favourite – that allows students to self-assess the key aspects of the lesson's learning in a totally different way. It is always very interesting to listen in as students discuss this, as almost inevitably the students will mention things that are far removed from what the teacher would expect to be the two key items. These 'unexpected responses' are very similar to the 'wrong answer' during a discussion; throwing a light on what might be areas of misunderstanding, lack of what was thought to be 'previous knowledge', or perhaps simply highlighting the importance of a particular definition that the teacher may not have stressed.

Finally, as a plenary exercise, that was always one that my students enjoyed very much.

4:5 Assessing work that has been peer or self-assessed

What *not* to do

Something that I have unfortunately witnessed on several occasions, when observing science lessons that have involved some form of peer or self-assessment, has been where the teacher ends the exercise by saying to the students, 'When I get the work in, I will mark it again properly.' In these cases, the teacher may as well have not even bothered with the peer or self-assessment exercise. After all, these teachers are making it perfectly clear to the students that what they are doing is not 'proper' assessment. As a teacher you should *never* make a statement like this, and you are probably thinking right now, well, obviously I would not do this. However, these 'don't worry, I will sort it all out later' comments are much more frequent than you may expect. Sometimes the language is not quite so blatant, but even saying, 'Don't worry, I will check it this evening' carries the same message: that the teacher will be the person who 'properly' assesses the work later.

Even if the teacher does not actually verbalise their intentions in this way, all too often they feel compelled to 'mark the work properly', giving full feedback as normal. This too undermines the whole point of peer or self-assessment and reduces the importance of the skill in the eyes of the students.

Use the peer or self-assessment to save time

When checking work that has been assessed by students, it is always best to start by reading the comments they have written rather than the work itself. Then have a quick look at the work to see if the comments seem reasonable. You do not have to be 100% in agreement but if, in general, you agree that learning objectives have been met, as stated, then a simple statement to note agreement is all that is required. For example:

'I agree with Matilda, I think you have obviously learned this work, Finley.'

Or

'I agree with you about both your learning objectives. Well done, Grace.'

These 'follow on' statements not only reinforce that the learning has been completed, but also reinforce that the peer or self-assessment was done well.

If, having read the peer or self-assessment comments and looked at the work, the teacher does not agree with what the student has written, then the 'follow on' comment this time should say so, say precisely *why* and suggest a way to *improve the learning*. For example:

'I disagree with what Toby said about your learning, because you have muddled your use of the words "atoms" and "molecules". I suggest that you rewrite the definitions of these two key words, then go back through the work and check each time that you have used them to see if you used the correct one, Samuel. If you need help to do this, please see me.'

Or

'I agree with you about the first learning objective, Lara, but I think to be certain of the second learning objective, you will need to add two more differences between 'groups' and 'periods' in the periodic table. If you need help to do this, please see me.'

As with the students, teachers will need to practise this skill of writing a 'follow on' comment, rather than re-assessing work that has been assessed by students. There is no doubt, however, that in time this will definitely *reduce the time* needed to assess work by the teacher; not to mention how impressed anybody inspecting the books would be to see such a high level of involvement of students in assessing learning, and interacting with their teacher, in the books.

Peer and self-assessment are vital skills for students to learn, and obviously not just for science. Like *all* skills, they need to be gradually developed and continually practised if they are to be of use. Science teachers are used to teaching graph skills or practical skills through repetition and gradual development, and it seems sensible to use exactly this approach to the development of peer and self-assessment.

Chapter 5

Linking summative and formative assessment

5:1 Introduction – assessment balance in science

If you have not already read the introduction to this book, then I suggest that you check the definitions of the terms **formative assessment** and **summative assessment** given on pages 14-15. The chapters up to this point have dealt exclusively with formative assessment, and the improvement in student learning. However, summative assessment – the measuring of achievement of students – is extremely common in science, with most students regularly completing tests, exams and even assessed practicals, etc.

In most science departments, unfortunately, these summative assessments dominate assessment of the students, with far too little use of formative assessment. What is interesting is that even when good-quality formative feedback, discussion work, etc. is adopted and used within a science department, when it comes to summative assessments, these are almost always treated as totally separate from the day-to-day learning of the students, and these assessments are not used in any formative way whatsoever. But why is this? Why is so much time invested in assessments that are *not* actually used to *improve learning* by the students? Why can't summative assessments be used formatively, in the same way that all the other work completed by students can?

Well, in actual fact it is pretty easy to do just that and to integrate the two assessment types, although for some reason this does not seem to occur to many science teachers. Hopefully the rest of this chapter will alter that outlook and make the most of the time spent on summative assessments to maximise progress in learning, as well as the *measuring* of that progress.

5:2 The ultimate assessment question

Before moving on, at this stage it is essential to address the million-pound assessment question. This is the *only* question you ever really need to ask students in order to find out if your summative assessments are already doing all that they should. As with all the best questions, it is nothing extraordinary or revolutionary in any way. Nor does it depend on the age or ability of the students, as the question can be used on *any* student. The question is used following a test or exam of some kind – a summative assessment – after which the student has been provided with their grade/level. All you need to ask is:

'If you received a grade/level ... in the test/exam, what would you have to do to get a higher grade/level in future?'

When I started teaching at my final school, my headteacher asked me to find out how well AfL was already working within the school across the whole curriculum. So, I simply asked this question, verbally, to a range of girls from Year 7 to 13, across the whole range of subjects. As the school was a very high-achieving girls' grammar, clearly the students had extremely good levels of verbal skills, therefore it would have been reasonable to expect a whole range of eloquent and differing answers, depending on age, ability, subject, etc. However, with the exception of art, in *every* subject, at all ages, the students always provided versions of just three basic answers:

'I will have to work harder.'

'I will have to revise better/more.'

'I can't improve. I am not clever/good enough at this subject.'

I have often repeated this million-pound question at other schools, with both genders and varying levels of ability. Despite the variety of students questioned, inevitably I have received the same results.

Interestingly, these same three basic answers are given in subjects such as science, which traditionally use little formative assessment, as well as in those such as English, in which formative assessment is much more likely to be intrinsically embedded within the work.

What is also interesting is that when pressed on each of these three basic answers, the students who describe the need to 'work harder' are rarely able to say what they will *actually* do. Some may say about concentrating more in class, not chatting, etc. but what actual work they might do when they 'work harder' is rarely mentioned.

For those students who answer that they need to 'revise more/better' when pressed to expand on this, there are some who admit they did not revise at all, or clearly did insufficient revision. However, for those students who clearly did revise, again they are almost never able to express exactly *how* they might improve their revision.

Finally, there are usually far too many students, regardless of age or scientific ability, who simply insist that they are 'unable to improve', as they seem to genuinely believe that their ability in a particular subject is fixed. Even with none-too-subtle prompts such as, 'Good job you didn't take this attitude when you started to learn to walk' or for older students, 'Well, that will be a tricky attitude when you start learning to drive,' even the most articulate students will often state that there is simply a limit to their abilities that they feel has been reached.

In reality, what these answers tell us is the fact that students, and in many cases, unfortunately, teachers too, separate these summative assessments from the day-to-day formative assessments. The tests or exams are seen to stand alone and to be divorced from other aspects of learning. As such, students do not usually see the same rules of *progress in learning* applying to their summative assessments. Look at the three basic student responses again. There is certainly nothing remotely *formative* about such statements.

It is the removal of this attitude of a separation between summative and formative assessment that I have particularly focused on developing over the years, since my first involvement on The King's College

Project, and I hope the remainder of this chapter will inspire you to do the same.

5:3 Revision and preparation for summative assessments

Regardless of age, gender or level of attainment, students clearly fall into two groups when it comes to revising for, and preparing for, tests: Those who do *some* revision/preparation, and those who do *none*. Surprisingly, the techniques that improve *both* groups, are simply variations of the same ideas. The reasons for this come from delving a little closer into these two student groups.

Students who do not revise for summative assessments

These can generally be subdivided into two main groups: Firstly, there are those students who 'can't be bothered' to revise or those who feel that there is 'no point'. Generally, these students tend to feel that they are unlikely to improve as a result of revision, as they see their potential as limited or fixed in some way. These are the students who usually provide the third of the three basic answers to the million-pound question mentioned above.

Alternatively, there are those students who feel that 'there is too much to learn' or that 'the bits I learn are never in the exams, anyway.' Both of these types of thought tend to reinforce in the students' minds that revision is not worth investing time in. They definitely do *not* see revising as a way of improving their overall *learning*, instead seeing it simply as a requirement in order to 'complete' their summative assessment.

Students who do revise

Students who do some revision tend to complain that 'the stuff I revise never appears in the test' or that 'I spent too much time on X, and not enough time on Y.' In both cases, these students seem to feel that there is a very random element to what they revise which may, or more likely may not, prove useful.

Sometimes students will realise that the amount or type of revision that they did was not suitable, but these tend to be quite generalised comments, and rarely are these students able to go on to say exactly *how* they will improve this in future, simply resorting to the second typical answer to the million-pound question: 'I will do more revision.'

One more problem that arises when looking more closely at students who do revise is that they tend to focus on one of two areas of their work: often, they spend a lot of time revising sections that they 'enjoy' most. In reality, this tends to usually mean that these are topics that they already understand and find less challenging, which is why they 'like' them. Thus, time is spent revising work that requires little time spent on it.

Alternatively, some students focus on sections of work that they really struggle with. Almost like some sort of martyrdom, some students will give huge amounts of time to something that 'they never really understood at all.' Often, this will result in relatively small, if any, gains in their knowledge and understanding, compared with the time invested.

From discussions with both groups of students, it is clear that despite the fact that all sorts of revision techniques are usually known and understood, it is the *volume* of knowledge and learning required in science that students are unable to deal with, and in particular, knowing *which parts* of the work to focus on for the *greatest benefit*.

Narrowing down what needs to be revised by using Smart Revision Sheets

One of the most important techniques that benefits students preparing for science tests or exams is for the students *themselves* to be able to select those areas of knowledge and understanding that they think they will most benefit from spending revision time on. I introduced **Smart Revision Sheets** that were used for Years 7-13 and at all abilities. I created these with the help of departmental colleagues, and I must especially thank Noel Sturt for his input into their final appearance. A KS3 and an A-level biology example of these sheets can be seen below.

P1.1- Forces Name: Date:

	Facts (These are facts that you just have to KNOW)	Date	Revision resource made	Confidence
	Traffic light these **facts**: GREEN – I already know, AMBER – okay once I've really thought about it/looked it up, and RED – I can't remember. Then focus on using **MEMORY TECHNIQUES** and **repetition** to learn the AMBER ones **first** and then the REDS.			
1.	A force is a push or a pull.			
2.	To measure forces you use a Newton metre.			
3.	Forces can change the shape of objects by compressing or extending them.			
4.	Hooke's law states that the extension of a piece of elastic doubles, when the force doubles.			
5.	The force of friction acts between two solid surfaces in contact that are sliding across each other.			
6.	The surfaces are rough and will grip each other.			
7.	Air resistance and water resistance are drag forces.			
8.	When a moving object contacts air or water particles it has to push them out of the way.			
9.	Forces that act at a distance are called non-contact forces.			
10.	The force of gravity acts on things that have mass.			
11.	Your mass is the amount of stuff you are made up of and is measured in grams.			
12.	Your weight is the force of gravity on an object and is measured in Newtons.			
13.	If forces acting on an object are the same size but in opposite directions they are balanced and said to be in equilibrium.			
14.	If forces acting on an object are not the same size they are unbalanced.			
15.	Unbalanced forces change the speed or direction of an object.			

	Processes (These are things you must be able to DO)	Revision resource made	Confidence
	Traffic light these **processes**: GREEN – I already know, AMBER – okay once I've really thought about it/looked it up, and RED – I don't understand. Then focus on using **MEMORY TECHNIQUES** and **repetition** to learn the AMBER ones **first** and then the REDS.		
1.	Identify interaction pairs acting on an object.		
2.	Explain when you compress a material, the bonds push back and generate a reaction force. When a book is sitting on a table gravity pulls the book down. The table pushes back on the book.		
3.	Identify the forces in a force diagram.		
4.	Identify types of drag forces.		
5.	Explain why it is easier for an object to go through air rather than water. Use the idea of particles.		
6.	Explain that your mass never changes but your weight can change depending on which planet you are on.		
7.	Be able to identify and explain the result of balanced and unbalanced forces on an object.		

Revision resources checked:

F212 Section 2.3.4 Maintaining biodiversity AfL sheet Name: Date:

Date learned	Resource made ✓	Facts (These are facts that you just have to KNOW)	Processes (These are things you must be able to DO)	Resource made ✓	Learning done ✓
		Traffic light these facts: GREEN – I already know, AMBER – okay once I've really thought about it/looked it up, and RED – I can't remember. Then focus on using **MEMORY TECHNIQUES** and repetition to learn the AMBER ones first and then the **REDS**.	Write revision notes for each one, using your notes, the textbook and the internet. Where possible, use a **THINKING MAP** to display your thinking in a clear and memorable way. Then focus on using **MEMORY TECHNIQUES** and repetition to learn the processes you didn't already know.		
		1. The **gene pool** for a species consists of all the genes present in all the individuals of the species – the fewer individuals, the smaller the gene pool.	• **Outline** reasons for the conservation of organisms, with reference to economic, ethical and aesthetic reasons.		
		2. **Genetic erosion** is the gradual loss of genetic diversity in a species.	• **Discuss** the consequences of global climate change on the biodiversity of organisms, with reference to changing patterns of agriculture and the spread of disease.		
		3. *In situ* conservation means conservation in the natural environment.	• **Explain** the benefits for agriculture of maintaining biodiversity of animal and plant species.		
		4. *Ex situ* conservation means conservation outside of the normal environment; such as zoos, botanical gardens, etc.	• **Describe** the conservation of endangered species, both *in situ*, and *ex situ*, with reference to the advantages and disadvantages of these two approaches.		
		5. **CITES** is the Convention in International Trade in Endangered Species – a worldwide agreement, first made in 1973.	• **Discuss** the role of botanic gardens in the *ex situ* conservation of rare plant species, or plant species extinct in the wild, with reference to seed banks.		
		6. The **Rio Convention on Biodiversity** was supported by many countries in 1992, and agreed to promote **sustainable development** in each country.	• **Discuss** the importance of international cooperation in species conservation, with reference to **CITES** and the **Rio Convention on Biodiversity**.		
		7. **Environmental impact assessments** assess the likely impact of a proposed development on the environment.	• **Discuss** the significance of environmental impact assessments for local authority planning decisions.		

133

Regardless of age or ability, all these Smart Revision Sheets had a similar style, with one sheet per topic or section of work. (With GCSE and higher qualifications, sometimes a sheet would extend over three or four sides of A4, but each side would contain the full headings shown above.) The sheets are divided into sections for **Key Facts** and **Processes**. At GCSE, A-level, IB, etc. the Processes statements were almost word-for-word what the exam board specification said was required from the students. At KS3 the Processes were similarly worded, but were internally generated by the science department. These Processes were the starting points when producing the sheets, as these were clearly what the students actually had to be able to do, in order to *progress in their learning*.

Linked to the Processes were a number of Key Facts that would be essential to know in order to be able to complete the process. So, in the enclosed A-level example, for a student to be able to '*describe* the conservation of endangered species, both *in situ* and *ex situ*, with reference to the advantages and disadvantages of these two approaches' which is mentioned in the Processes column, they would clearly need to know the definition of the two terms 'in situ' and 'ex situ' that are listed in the Key Facts column. Obviously, it is not possible for *every* fact to be included on such a sheet, but the lists of Key Facts meant that students could readily see reminders of some of the most important information required.

Smart Revision Sheets in daily use

The students would receive a copy of their Smart Revision Sheet whenever they *started* a new topic or section of work. This had a number of benefits. Firstly, students were able to see the overall learning aims of the whole topic and the amount of work to be covered. Some topics, for example, might need three sides of A4, whereas others might only need one.

Another benefit of having the sheets at the *start* of a unit of work, was that the students sometimes recognised facts that they already knew. For example, the speed = distance/time triangle might appear on a sheet in GCSE physics, having already been learned at KS3. This had the advantage of showing students how learning *builds* on previous learning, and could also mean that for some students they would enter a new unit realising that they already knew some of the key information, which was obviously a boost for their confidence.

The final advantage of having the sheets at the start of the unit was that the students saw them as a *working* document, which had the benefit of the students also seeing the revision at the end of the unit as a continuation of their everyday 'work', rather than something separate from it.

In each lesson, the teacher would ask students to date the relevant Key Facts and Processes as they were covered. The importance of having a date on the students' own classwork also became more relevant, rather than being just something else that the teacher 'nagged' about. This meant that when looking back during revision, students were readily able to see when they actually covered the relevant work in class. It also formed a link between the lesson's learning objectives and the Processes, which were required for future tests or exams. Once more, this reinforced the fact that work done in class or at home was essential for future success, and continuing the theme of a *language of learning*.

Using Smart Revision Sheets before a summative assessment test or exam

When a test or exam on the relevant topic was imminent, students would be asked, either as a home learning task or during a lesson, to **traffic light** each of the Key Facts and Processes on the sheet. Usually they would do this using highlighters or coloured pencils. This is explained on the examples provided, but is as follows:

Green – Key Fact or Process that I am sure I know/remember/ understand/can do.

Amber – Key Fact or Process that I sort of know/remember/ understand/can do.

Red – Key Fact or Process that I do not know/remember/ understand/cannot do.

Looking back at how students who *do* revise usually tackle revision – see page 130 – it is clear that too often they tend to focus their time on either the green or red items. The advantage of these sheets was that they could be used to 'force' students to tackle the *amber* Key Facts and Processes. This is the section of work, often ignored by students, that can actually bring the biggest benefit in terms of *learning gains* per unit of time spent revising.

There is no doubt that many students, especially the more motivated ones, will need to be 'forced' to tackle the amber sections first; often insisting that they need to tackle their red sections first. As with most ideas in this book, it is important to *continually train* the students to accept that the amber sections will bring most rewards. Most students will readily accept that too much time spent 'learning' items highlighted green is clearly not the best use of their time. Emphasising the importance of converting amber sections into green, rather than struggling to convert red into amber, is what is important. Looking at the definitions of these pairs (above), it should be reasonably easy to convince students that it is far better to be 'certain' (green) of more learning, than to 'sort of know' (amber) more learning.

With motivated students who *do* usually revise, experience shows that they quickly realise the benefit of tackling their amber sections. This not only gives the students focus for revision, but also eliminates many of their concerns about revising things that are not needed, or about the sheer *volume* of 'stuff' that needs revising for science. Suddenly, instead of having to revise the whole sheet's worth of information, they may only need to tackle half of it. The boost that this gives these students is huge.

For those students who *do not* usually revise, the sheets can be used in a slightly different way. They can be used to show that even *small* amounts of revision can make a difference. With students like these, it may be that they are asked, for example, to select any one (or whatever number is deemed appropriate) Key Fact or Process that they highlighted as amber, and convert it to green, by carefully focusing their revision on that alone. For this group of students, it is equally empowering to realise that (a) they *can* actually revise and remember more than they already knew, and (b) they can see that revision is not just about 'learning everything' or there being 'too much', but instead is a number of small, *manageable* steps. Surely it is far better if those students with the least motivation and drive are encouraged over a few weeks to learn, say, five key pieces of information, even if it leaves a lot of learning not done, than to revert to them learning nothing at all. Both students and teachers will be surprised at how much difference such seemingly small 'gains' in learning make in summative assessments, not to mention – even more importantly – the difference in attitude this can result in with students reluctant to the whole concept of revision.

Ideally, both groups of students should be allowed to decide *for themselves* which of their amber Key Facts or Processes they target, and in which order. However, they should always be encouraged to do their 'easiest' ones first. This will mean that they make most progress with their *earliest* revision, which will, hopefully, tend to encourage the students to continue.

Dealing with red Key Facts or Processes

Inevitably some students, especially the more motivated ones, will be concerned by the Key Facts and Processes that they have highlighted red, indicating a complete lack of understanding. There are a number of ways to tackle these.

Firstly, it is important for students to realise, and to be told, that they *never* need to know 100% of the work they have learned in science. At any level, a score of 80-90% will almost certainly guarantee the highest test/exam grade. So, if a student has just the odd Key Fact or Process that is red from a very long list, this can easily be put into perspective.

Another valuable way of dealing with red highlights is to encourage students to see these as areas for tackling, not alone, but with the help of others. This could be a friend, but could also be during class or extracurricular revision sessions. Students could support each other by pairing a student who has marked a Key Fact or Process red with one who has marked it green, for example.

All too often science teachers select which topics will be revised during class revision sessions, often based on historical evidence which may, or may not, be relevant to the current students. Instead, this information should come *from the students*. For example, if almost all the students in the group have highlighted a particular Process in red, that would suggest it would be a very good idea to spend time revisiting this work in class. Checking this level of information is very quickly and easily done by the teacher during a lesson, if necessary. Alternatively, workstations could be set up during a revision session, where help sheets, past exam questions to practise, etc. are provided for particular red Key Facts or Processes at different locations within the room.

Finally, revision sessions either during or outside scheduled lessons could be provided with focus on particular areas of the topic. For example, there may be lessons or revision sessions being offered where

Mr X might be covering the first five Processes, Miss Y, the second five Processes, and Mrs Z the final five Processes. In this way, students could opt to join the session most beneficial for their *own* needs.

Whichever technique is used to deal with red Key Facts or Processes, it is essential that the students and teachers see these problems as individual steps that can be helped with *targeted* support.

Making full use of Smart Revision Sheets

There are a few other columns on the Smart Revision Sheets that can also be used to help the students to prepare for their exams. Both for the Key Facts and the Processes, there is a column that can be ticked to show that a revision resource has actually been made by the student.

For those students who *do* usually produce revision materials, this can be a useful tool for both the student and the teacher to keep track of the progress of production of materials. A teacher may, for example, check the revision resources and use the sheet to compare what has actually been done with what the student says has been done. Similarly, the teacher or student may put a date, rather than just a tick, by each resource as it is completed or checked.

Another benefit of this 'resource made' column, is that students can use the sheet to be more precise about their tasks in their revision timetable; for example, 'This week I will produce revision resources for the five Processes marked amber in the topic on X' rather than just 'Make some science resources.' Again, it is all about improving the students' *language of learning*.

For those students who *do not* usually produce revision resources, the sheets can be used to encourage their production in very small steps, in a similar manner as was mentioned earlier. For example: 'This week, select any five amber Key Facts and produce a revision aid to help you learn them.' This gives the students ownership over *which* Key Facts they produce revision materials for while focusing on only a small number of facts, which the students will see as more manageable. By focusing on amber Key Facts, the students will avoid using their time unproductively.

The final column on the Smart Revision Sheets is titled 'learning done' (or 'confidence'). This column can be used in two ways. Firstly, students can individually tick off Processes when they are confident that they have actually *learned* them. Alternatively, the column can be revisited later following the test/exam. This will be covered later in this topic on page 153, but basically involves students reflecting on whether or not they had actually learned what they thought they had.

As I said earlier, variations of these sheets have been used across the whole age and ability range, from simplified ones using smiley faces, and with more Key Facts and less Processes, to ones at the highest level, as in the A-level biology example shown. By encouraging students to always work on a *limited number* of *targeted* sections of work for their revision, these sheets have proven to be both incredibly successful and very popular, with both students and teachers, as a method for helping students to prepare in a more formative manner for their summative tests.

5:4 Making a summative test or exam paper more formative

Having encouraged students to prepare for tests and exams in a more structured and 'smart' manner, all internal tests and exams in science had a cover that was as far removed from the traditional 'name, mark, grade' look as it could be. Looking at the example of a KS3 test cover and one from a typical GCSE biology test below, it is abundantly clear to any student or teacher looking at it that this test is about so much more than simply obtaining a grade.

Using the tests to move away from being stand-alone summative assessments to being part of the ongoing formative assessment of the students learning is highlighted by the variety of information on, and multiple uses of, this test cover. As with the Smart Revision Sheets (page 131), these test covers have been adapted and used for all abilities and across Years 7 to 13.

Over the next pages, each of the features of the test cover will be explained. However, one quick thing to note is that even if given a title, these covers *never* used the word 'test' – 'summative assessment' is much better, and helps the students to realise that it is just another part of the jigsaw of assessment.

Year 7 End of Topic Assessment			**P1.1- Forces**

Name:	Group:	Date:

Instructions:
- **Answer all questions. You may use a calculator.**
- **Time allowed: 20 minutes**

Qu.	Topic	Marks available	Predicted mark	Actual mark	
1	Forces	6			
2	Mass and weight	3			
3	Gravitational field strength	4			
4	Forces	3			
5	Reaction forces	2			
6	Applying your forces knowledge	2			%
	Total	20			

Feedback:

WWW Teacher: ....

WWW Student: ....

Maths or graphical error	Application of knowledge	Not Reading question carefully	Clarity and precision of answer	Knowledge not revised/ understood	Statements per mark

EBI	Teacher:
	Student:

Student response:
....
....
....
....
....

Year 9 Biology			Target Grade:	
B1-2 Summative assessment				
Name:		Group:	Date:	

Timing: 45 minutes

Unit	Qu.	Topic	Marks available	Predicted mark	Actual mark	
B1	1	Cell structure	4			
	2	Diffusion and oxygen	5			
	3	Size and root adaptation	6			
B2	4	Fat digestion (QWC)	6			
	5	Enzymes (data)	5			
	6	Heart	5			
	7	Blood vessels	5			
	8	Alveoli adaptations	3			
	9	Circulation and exercise	6			**Grade**
		Total	**45**			

Feedback:

WWW Teacher: ....

WWW Student: ....

Maths or graphical error	Application of knowledge	Not Reading question carefully	Clarity and precision of answer	Knowledge not revised/ understood	Statements per mark

EBI	Teacher:
	Student:

Student response:

....

....

....

....

Instant self-reflection on tests and exams

One key aspect of this bridging of summative and formative assessment was that all internal science tests were made to a time length that allowed for ten minutes of time at the end of the assessment, during which students would do an *instant appraisal* of the test to determine their confidence with it. This was not done overall for the whole test, but by asking students to estimate their score on each question in the **predicted mark** column of the first table on the front cover. This 10-minute period of self-reflection was done with all tests and exams in science, from KS3 to A-level.

For students of lower age/attainment this column was altered slightly, so that each question was given a 'traffic light':

Green – I am confident I scored most/all marks on this question

Amber – I feel that I have got some of this question correct

Red – I do not think I have scored any/many marks on this question.

For some students, smiley, sad and 'in between' faces were used as an alternative to the three colours, but with the same meanings.

At higher levels of age/attainment students would be expected to look through their answers and estimate how many marks they would gain on each question. This had to be only one figure, not 6-8 or 5½, etc. In KS4 and KS5, estimates were often required for *parts* of a question, to be even more precise, especially if the test itself was shorter – for example, a mid-topic test.

One other thing to notice is that when students were completing this task, on the front cover there appeared not only the question numbers, but also the relevant topic content. This may be vague, such as 'sound and light' for a simple Year 7 exam, to being really precise, such as 'topic C4b – The halogens' at higher levels. In both cases, the front cover highlighted *actual* topics of work that might have gained/lost marks. Having this information on the test cover also helped to directly link actual pieces of classwork or revision to specific questions in the summative assessment.

Getting students to instantly reflect on their answers to each question in this manner has a number of benefits.

Firstly, it is possible for the teacher to see questions, topics, types of question, etc. that the whole class are generally more/less confident with. This can be even more valuable once the actual marks for these questions are awarded. It may mean that there are topics/types of question that students clearly are generally good at that can be removed from future revision sessions, or alternatively, if students seem confident on questions that they generally score badly at, or vice versa, then more in-depth analysis may be needed to find out why there is this disparity. In both cases, this is extremely useful information for the teacher when looking at the bigger picture on learning progress with a *whole group* of students.

The second benefit of this instant reflection is for the students themselves. When students have their papers returned, they are able to compare their predicted scores/confidence with their actual results for each question. This can highlight many useful things. It may show students that they are actually better at certain topics/skills than they think – or not! For example, it seems that many students often worry about answers involving maths or graphs, and as a result they may predict these results lower because of a lack of confidence with maths, which may turn out to be incorrect as their mathematics ability may be fine for their needs in science.

Another benefit to students comes when they compare their confidence with answers and their actual score with their confidence in topics on their Smart Revision Sheets (page 131). Students may find that topics that they expected to do well/badly on may or may not have gone as expected. This can prove useful for the students to help them to move their revision and preparation forward for future summative assessments.

Finally, a benefit of asking students to instantly reflect on how well, or not, they thought each question went also has the benefit of making students realise that the single, overall grade is not *all* that is important in this summative assessment, reinforcing the overall message that the test is an assessment to help with future *progress in learning*.

Helping students to improve their MARCKS

One obvious addition to a more traditional science test cover is the second table that has the following information in it:

Maths or graphical error	Application of knowledge	Not Reading question carefully	Clarity and precision of answer	Knowledge not revised/ understood	Statements per mark
EBI	Teacher:				

This came about after myself and a science colleague, with whom I had been developing the use of AfL in science, had both been moaning about how many marks students lost in exams by not reading the questions. After looking through many papers, it was clear that scientific knowledge alone was not *all* that lost students marks, and that there were other key exam skills that were major contributors to lost marks. After doing more analysis of various science assessments, across the three sciences and at all ages, we settled on five areas on top of lack of scientific knowledge that caused students to regularly lose marks. With a little work, and the help of Vicki Sharp, the head of physics, these were formed into the acronym **MARCKS**, which stood for the following:

M – **M**athematical or graphical skill.

A – **A**pplication of knowledge (rather than direct recall of facts – especially in physics).

R – Failure to **R**ead the question carefully.

C – Lack of **C**larity and precision in terminology, etc. (especially in biology).

K – Lack of the scientific **K**nowledge needed to answer the question.

S – Not writing enough separate **S**tatements to gain the number of required marks. (This was particularly pertinent in biology, where three- or four-mark questions often need three or four separate, specific points.)

It was decided to focus on these six areas across the age and attainment range, so the table above was added to the front cover of *all* science summative assessments.

When teachers marked these summative assessments, if an answer was correct, the work was given a tick, as normal. However, if an answer was wrong, a teacher would, instead of putting a cross, put one or more of the **MARCKS** letters. It is important to realise that a single mark answer could be given two or more of these letters. For example, if a student had made an error in a maths calculation, it may have been a **M**aths skill problem – **M** – or it may have been due to misreading the figures in the question – **R**. In this case, the teacher may put both letters by the single incorrect answer. The student would later be able to decide which was the reason for the wrong answer – maybe both!

When this was first introduced, some staff immediately said that this would 'take longer to mark' and this may well be your first thought too. However, very quickly, it was found that this was definitely *not* the case. Firstly, teachers quite quickly start to realise which letters are most likely to be associated with particular questions/answers. Secondly, it saves teachers spending time highlighting parts of the question and writing 'Read this' or the equivalent, or writing phrases such as, 'Use a calculator' or 'Three separate answers needed'.

I can honestly say that in more than 15 years since this **MARCKS** concept was first introduced, *none* of the teachers who have used this system of marking tests and exams have found it takes any more time than 'normal' marking. Indeed, on several occasions, teachers who had been used to this system found it so much quicker and easier, that they naturally continued using it, even after moving to other schools who had never heard of it! You will, I'm afraid, simply have to take my word on this, although one easy way to find out of course, would be to try it out. I *guarantee* that within a year, the teachers will be taking *less time* marking summative assessments. And if that is not an added bonus, then I don't know what is!

When the paper has been marked and has been returned to the student, the students themselves complete a tally chart of their total number of **M**, **A**, **R**, **C**, **K** and **S** errors on the table on the cover of the assessment (in the spaces underneath each of the skills in the second table.)

In most instances, most students will have more **K** – scientific **K**nowledge – errors than anything else. However, students are often surprised to see just how many marks were lost *not* through their scientific **K**nowledge, but through other exam or related skills. For example, at the girls' grammar school where I finished my career, despite their high levels of English, many girls lost marks due to not

Reading the questions carefully enough, especially (but not only) in biology. When investigating this further, it turned out that the girls were used to skim reading material that served them well in many areas of their education, but clearly not when it came to reading science exam questions. Such information was vital, both for the students themselves and their science teachers, in developing their learning and improving their final grades.

Maths or graphical errors would be used to highlight mistakes in calculations, plotting of graphs, not labelling axes, allocating the axes the wrong way around, misuse of or missing units, etc. As was mentioned earlier, it may be that if a student uses the incorrect units, this is because of a **M**athematical error, or it could be by poor **R**eading of the question, in which case both skill errors **M** and **R** could be indicated.

By highlighting that these are **M**athematical errors and not scientific **K**nowledge errors, this helps students to see that (a) their revision of scientific knowledge was not at fault for these lost marks, and that (b) revision time may need to be allocated to specifically work on these relevant maths skills.

Application of knowledge errors were particularly common in physics, but were also found in biology and chemistry. These would occur when students failed to realise that science they had learned using one specific example could be **A**pplied to other examples. For example, if a student had learned that the moon had a lower gravity because of its smaller mass, and that Jupiter had a larger gravity because of its larger mass, if a student was then unable to estimate the gravity of another planet, based on its size, this would show that despite the scientific **K**nowledge being learned, the student was unable to **A**pply this knowledge.

This ability of transferring scientific **K**nowledge to new situations is clearly vital but is rarely seen as a separate and important skill, despite the fact that it is often responsible for students losing marks in summative assessments.

Not **Reading the question** carefully is often costly for students doing summative assessments in science. As mentioned earlier, this is not only an issue for those students with low language skills or reading ages. When working with this issue with students who had very good reading abilities, it was interesting to see the number of issues that arose. For example, many students it seems, simply 'miss' or ignore an introductory sentence or two before an image, graph, diagram, etc. at the very start of a question. When asked about this, the students often say that they assume this introductory sentence to be unimportant!

Another issue, as mentioned above, is that if the question has a lot of information to read students may 'skim' through to 'get on to the question quickly'.

Another point that arose from working with students to eradicate errors in **R**eading questions, was the fact that most students did not appreciate the difference between these two different starts to questions:

Version 1

Q1 (a) The halogens are an important group of elements in the periodic table:

(i) Name an element from this group that is a gas.

Version 2

Q1 The halogens are an important group of elements in the periodic table.

(a) (i) Name an element from this group that is a gas.

Even students with high reading and science ability did not appreciate that in the first example, only the questions in part (a) of Q1 would be relevant to the halogens, whereas, in the second example, questions in parts (b), (c), etc. of Q1 would also be about the halogens. This ability to be able to 'decode' examination questions is not something that students just acquire as they become older, but is a skill that actually needs *teaching*. Clearly, however, in both of these examples, if a student had named a chemical element that was a gas, but which was not a halogen, this could be due to a lack of scientific **K**nowledge, but equally could have been due to not **R**eading the question carefully. A surprising number of students will actually start reading this question with the word 'name...' as they see this as 'the question' rather than an introduction to the question.

The **Clarity and precision** mark would usually show the *incorrect* use of scientific terminology; for example, confusing the terms hypothermia and hyperthermia, or for saying 'protein' when what was required was 'globular protein', or 'metal' when what was required was 'group 1 metal'. Another example would be when students failed to actually use a particular scientific word that was required by the mark scheme, despite describing the word, such as when a student writes 'materials that did not conduct electricity' but fails to use the word 'insulators'. In all these cases, it is clear that the students do, indeed, have the correct scientific **K**nowledge, but their actual choice of words, or the *precision* of the words chosen, has lost them marks.

Clarity and precision issues often highlighted students who would 'waffle' in their answers. A particular issue in biology seems to be that many students use words such as 'them' or 'they', feeling that it is 'obvious' what they are writing if the examiner rereads the question. Work is often required by teachers to get students to realise that (a) examiners will *not* reread the question and (b) even if the examiner did reread the question, which 'them' the student was referring to was still not always clear. So, for example, if a question mentions red and white blood cells, if the student refers to one of the cell types as 'them', it may be unclear to the examiner which cell type they actually mean.

Knowledge not revised or understood is almost certainly going to be the most common loss of marks by most students. However, it is important that is *not* seen simply as 'did not revise'. Students need to realise that it may be the lack of detail in their revision, or the muddling of information that they clearly *have* revised that could lose them marks. Thus, it is important as a teacher to make it clear that this is the skill that you would expect students to lose most marks on. However, it should also be made clear that there may be different solutions for different students when trying to make progress in this area. What is vital is that the students do not become disheartened, and simply give up revising or preparing for summative assessments. For some students, especially those lacking confidence in their scientific ability, I have even encouraged them to ignore this section, initially, and concentrate on the other five skills that they often see as 'more attainable' as ways of making progress. Only when they have boosted their confidence by making progress with the other skills, would I then move on to tackle their lack of scientific **K**nowledge.

Often very interesting is the **Statements per mark** skill that forces students to realise that repeating the question in the answer – something that turned out to be very common – does *not* actually gain any marks, despite 'filling the answer space', which many – especially younger or less able – students seem to feel is what is required of them. Indeed, you may be surprised to discover just how many older and more able students still assume that if they write one answer long enough to fill the required space, then they must stand a chance of gaining the required three or four marks. Again, especially, although not exclusively, in biology, students will need to be *trained* to understand that often each mark is for a *separate* mark point allocated by the examiner, thus three marks will often mean three, separate **S**tatements.

By highlighting these individual skills for individual students, the exam feedback became so much more than simply a grade. Students and teachers were able to use the two tables on the front of the test with the marks per question, the topic information and the exams skills **MARCKS** to reflect *in detail* on how best individuals and whole groups should progress with their learning, thus changing the information provided by the *summative* assessment into a form of *formative* feedback that was useful for progress in learning.

Using MARCKS information with whole teaching groups

As a teacher, if it becomes clear that a particular skill, such as **C**larity and precision or **S**tatements per mark, is generally causing problems with a group of students, it follows that future work should target these skill areas. So, for example, the teacher may provide starters to lessons that consist of vague sentences and ask students to improve their **C**larity and precision. This could be as simple as providing the students with copies of wrong answers from past papers that lacked **C**larity. Another tip is to make use of the 'additional guidance' provided with exam mark schemes. Often these will say that an answer must use a particular word or phrase, and that an alternative word or phrase is *not* acceptable. In these instances, I suggest you use the words or phrase that the examiners say are not acceptable in starter sentences and get students to correct them. I have also used whole past exam papers, with some answers correct, others worded deliberately to lack **C**larity and precision, others with **M**aths or graphical errors, others with errors in **R**eading the questions, etc. The students really enjoy the challenge of marking these, and they would use MARCKS when marking them without being asked to do so, to find the errors before then correcting answers where necessary. Both at GCSE and A-level students found these really useful. Several students commented on how this exercise made them realise how important **C**larity was, for example, and how difficult it was deciding if an unclear answer was worthy of a mark.

Alternatively, home learning tasks or plenaries can be selected to focus on specific skill areas. So, if **M**athematics and graphical errors have been costing many students marks, practising these during lesson plenaries, or as home learning tasks would obviously be beneficial.

It is also possible for the teacher to give the students some *choice* in their progress. For example, for home learning there may be a choice whereby students can select which three tasks they wish to complete out of three tasks focusing on **M**aths and graphical skills, three on the need to **R**ead questions carefully, and three on the need to be **C**lear and precise with answers. This is a particularly powerful learning tool as it emphasises the fact that home learning is something that will directly benefit the students *as individuals*. It is also interesting how often these types of home learning, where a choice is provided, are more often completed by even reluctant students.

Lessons (particularly 'revision' lessons) aimed at particular MARCKS skills will not only be beneficial to improving student grades, but will provide a break from the continued focus on recall and understanding of scientific **K**nowledge that some students find off-putting.

Using MARCKS for feedback for all assessments

Once introduced and used for summative assessments by teachers, it quickly became apparent that many staff were using MARCKS when assessing *all* other student work. Teachers would put the appropriate MARCKS letters in the margins of work and would refer to them when providing 'Even Better If...' written feedback. Quickly, MARCKS went from being a very useful feedback tool for summative assessments, to a very useful feedback tool for *all* science assessments. It makes sense if you think about it, as the students are very likely to make the same type of skill errors in their class or home learning tasks as they are in summative assessments.

Large posters with the MARCKS information on were displayed in all the science labs (here, I must admit, it helps having a wife who works as a graphic designer at a printers!).

How to

your examination skills

When you are answering, check your...

Maths and Graphical skills

Application of knowledge

Clarity and Precision of sentences
No 'it', 'them' or 'they' - correct scientific words

Knowledge
Make sure you have revised in enough detail

Statements per mark
One bullet point for each mark

©P. Spenceley

What Went Well and Even Better If...

Two other pieces of information on the front of the test are directly in line with other written feedback (see chapter 3). This continues the idea that the *summative assessment* is no different to any other piece of work in science, in that its purpose is to provide guidance for improvement in learning. So, in the same way as with other pieces of written feedback, the test has opportunities for providing two pieces of information on **What Went Well**, and one piece of guidance on **Even Better If...**.

As with other written feedback, the 'What Went Well' statements provided by the teacher should be simple and factual. For example, 'You did well on the questions on the heart' or 'You have fewer issues with **C**larity and precision than on your last test.'

Depending on circumstances, in some cases the teacher would complete *both* of these 'What Went Well' statements, or alternatively the student would complete one or maybe even both of them. There is more information about involving the students in this process opposite.

These short, factual 'What Went Well' statements, in line with everyday written feedback, address all the issues associated with written feedback that were covered in chapter 3, but often come up when teachers feel obliged to 'write something' on the front of a test/exam cover. They remove the gratuitous 'well done' or other ego-boosting, uninformative statements too often seen, or the 'could do better' or other uninformative, negative statements that are also very common. They also continue the *language of learning* that both teachers and students should be familiar with.

Let's be honest here: it can sometimes be difficult to say something that 'went well' for some students on a summative assessment. However, by using the precise question information and skill information on the front cover, there should be something specific to write on every paper. Even if it ends up being, 'You answered all of question one.'

Even better if... statements could be based on scientific **K**nowledge. For example, 'Even better if you could describe the route of blood through the heart **by** learning the names of the parts of the heart.'

Alternatively, these statements may be linked to another skill. For example, '**Even better if** you had remembered to write one statement per mark for two- and three-mark questions.'

Students using the summative assessment to improve their own learning

The most important aspect of bringing summative and formative assessments closer together is undoubtedly the fact that such summative assessments should be used formatively *by the students*. With the amount of information provided on the front of the test, there are a variety of ways in which the students can use this productively.

Predicted marks compared with actual marks

One thing that students can do with their test is to look closely at the marks that they *predicted* themselves immediately on completion of the test, compared with their *actual* marks, using the information in the first table. This can be done in terms of a simple numbers exercise, or students could, for example, look through the paper at the MARCKS next to their answers to see *why* they lost marks that they expected to score. This may mean that a student notices that rather than a **K**nowledge of particular topics costing them marks, it may have been a particular skill that was the issue, such as problems with their **M**aths or graphical skills.

As touched on earlier, students could be asked to do a three-way reflection, comparing their predicted marks with their actual marks and their Smart Revision Sheets (see page 132-133). This is particularly important for questions where students have lost marks because of their **K**nowledge of science. This could, for example, simply highlight to a student that they were correct when they flagged up a particular topic as requiring help when revising (red traffic light on the Smart Revision Sheet). Or, alternatively, it may highlight an overconfidence with a particular topic that a student felt they had revised and understood, and have discovered this not to be the case. Clearly, in both circumstances, the student finds out something very useful from this exercise.

Traffic lighting the Smart Revision Sheet again at this stage may be useful, where students are allowed to award traffic lights as follows. For example, (obviously percentage figures may vary as appropriate):

Green – I got 70% or more of the answers on this topic correct.

Amber – I got 50-69% of the answers on this topic correct.

Red – I got less than 50% of the answers to the questions on this topic correct.

Setting personal targets

The **Student Response** section on the front of the test can be used to set specific targets for improvement. These could be left for the students to decide, or prescribed to them in some manner, depending on age, scientific ability and confidence with self-assessment skills (see chapter 4).

For example, younger students or those with lower attainment may be asked to suggest 'one *topic* that needs improved revision resources, and one *skill* that needs to be improved by practice.' In these instances, I have seen students write things such as, 'I will make a new revision resource on the heart with a better labelled diagram. I will check my home learning and replace words like 'them' and 'they' with science words to improve my clarity.' Clearly, this will depend on the students' confidence in, and training with, self-assessment.

More experienced students, particularly those who have developed their self-assessment skills, could be given more choice about the areas that they wish to improve. This brings to mind an example of a high-achieving A-level student who, following her biology mock, noticed that she did well on short-answer questions that had only one or two marks, requiring factual recall. She also noticed that she had done well on longer answer questions, requiring many related facts and explanations. However, having realised she had received a number of **S**tatement per mark errors, and by looking at her predicted and actual marks, she realised that three- and four-mark questions were where she tended to lose marks, often dropping one or two of those available. Her Student Response task, which she carried out successfully, was 'to do all the three- and four-mark questions from every past paper available.' Her final A* grade clearly reflected the benefit of such a detailed Student Response to an exam! The chances of her ever realising this level of detail was required to improve her result, if she had simply been provided with her paper and a grade A, were beyond remote.

What is most important with the Student Response section is that it should be clear and precise about *exactly* what is required for the student to make progress in their learning, and thus their final grade.

Small steps – progress with those lacking motivation

One very successful feature of providing detailed feedback to students on the cover of their summative assessment, is how it can open up progress to students who have low attainment and those who often have low levels of self-esteem in science. Traditionally, these students receive back a test or exam that simply reflects, and indeed *reinforces*, their own lack of confidence with the subject. As a Year 10 student, receiving a summative assessment with simply a grade such as '4' can be not only demoralising, but can also feed into a vicious circle of further underachievement.

Providing more detailed feedback and information on the *next grade boundary* can often make these students realise that progress is not as far out of reach as they may feel. For example, if students are provided with the grade boundaries in terms of *actual marks* (rather than percentages, which most find difficult to understand), they are often surprised at how few actual marks are required to move to the next grade. If this is coupled with their MARCKS information, it is amazing how quickly even students with low expectations realise that a few small errors have cost them a grade.

One highly successful example of this was with a Year 11 group that had many students who had poor attainment and lacked motivation and self-belief in science. It happened to be an all-girls comprehensive, although similar groups obviously exist in many schools. Traditionally, when returning marked papers to a group such as this, the teacher would 'go over the test', allowing the students to correct answers. As an exercise, this is of extremely limited use to say the least, in terms of improving such students' learning.

Using the **small steps** technique with this group when their science mock exams had been marked – using MARCKS – and returned to the students, they were also provided with the grade boundaries as actual marks. The students were then given the **S**tudent **R**esponse task of making 'enough corrections to the paper to ensure that at least the next grade up was achieved'. The students were then allowed to use revision resources and their textbooks, but not other students or their own classwork, to make the improvements. By saying, 'at least the next grade' this meant that if a student was only one or two marks from the next grade, they could be encouraged to aim to improve by two grades. The idea of this task was to encourage the students to realise that, firstly, the next grade may be much closer in terms of actual correct answers than they might imagine, and secondly, to use the MARCKS information to notice how it may have been other skills rather than science **K**nowledge that had stopped them from gaining the next grade.

What quickly became obvious when this was done was that different students adopted completely different approaches to improvement, depending on the information on the front of their assessments. Some students realised that **M**aths or graphical errors had cost them 'easy' marks, and, for example, used a calculator to target these. Other students realised they had not **R**ead the question carefully, and targeted these for improvement. Other students realised that particular topic **K**nowledge had let them down. For example, the girl who used a diagram of the heart to pick up three additional marks, and with this, her next grade.

Their teacher was amazed not only at the responses of the students, but also by their engagement in the task (more on this in chapter 6). The students, however, were equally amazed to see how little was often needed to improve their success in science. As a motivational tool this exercise was *superb*. As a method of progressing student learning, it was also extremely useful – infinitely more so than 'going through the paper'.

Improvement by small steps became the buzzwords following this summative (mock exam) assessment and became the focus for a whole science revision program. This involved all Year 11 students having their science revision sessions divided into groups of three lessons.

The first lesson involved the students producing (in most cases) or updating revision resources on a particular topic(s). This topic was usually chosen by the teacher for the whole group, as this group was unfamiliar with the use of Smart Revision Sheets.

The second lesson involved the students completing some past GCSE exam questions, in exam conditions, specifically on the selected topic(s) with enough time left after the test in order for the students to complete an instant self-reflection, estimating how many marks they thought they would score on each question. The tests were then marked by the teacher (on occasion, the first lesson of the next 'triplet' would be completed next, in order to give the teacher enough time to mark the papers).

In the third lesson, the students used their marked work and MARCKS feedback to make *small* steps improvement to their exam answers and to their revision resources, if necessary. (Sometimes, the improvements to revision resources were completed as home learning tasks.)

This style of revision proved very popular with the students, not just because of the uniformity of approach, but also because the students were able to see clear evidence that they, as individuals, were making progress in the learning.

The success of these revision sessions was not only notable by the improvement in the cohort's exam results that summer, which saw the biggest jump in science results for several years, but also in the change in motivation and application of the students. As one teacher put it, 'They changed from hating science and insisting they were rubbish at it, to becoming almost obsessed about their next "small step" and the progress they were making. The difference was simply amazing.'

As with MARCKS (see page 151) there were **small steps** posters produced that were displayed in each of the science labs to reinforce the message, such as the example below.

5:5 Other ways to make summative assessments more formative

Several other successful techniques can be used in order to make summative assessments more formative, which have been used both for tests and exams, and other shorter summative assessments, such as write-ups of core practicals. In all cases, formative techniques were used that 'forced' the students to consider their work, and the quality of it, in comparison with what was actually required. The following are examples of techniques used.

Marking without a mark scheme

This technique has been used particularly successfully with end of topic tests, especially at KS3, but has been used very successfully throughout the age and attainment range – and not only in science.

Traditionally, it is quite common for students to complete end of unit tests in one lesson, and then in the following lesson, for the teacher to 'go through the answers', during which the students may or may not be asked to mark their own or somebody else's test, or to make corrections to their answers.

This technique involved the second lesson being used in a different, more formative, way. In the lesson after completing the test, the students may have kept their own test paper or may have swapped with other students in their group. The students would then be asked to work in a small group of perhaps three or four and to use a *pencil* to mark a small section of the work, for example, the first two pages. However, the students would not have been provided with a mark scheme. Instead, any marks awarded had to be agreed by consensus within the group.

I can still remember the first time that I asked a mixed-ability Year 7 group to do this. They looked aghast and said things like, 'How will we know if the answers are right or not?' I explained that I was sure there would be some answers that their group would all agree were correct. With some questions, some students may have different answers, in which case each student would have to *justify* their answer, and why they think it should get a mark. Finally, if it was impossible to decide if an answer should gain a mark or not, then after each marked section the students could explain what the problem was and why they were unsure if the answer deserved a mark or not, and the teacher would clear up any confusion.

It must be stressed that this process only works well if only a *small* section of the paper is tackled each time, before the teacher then provides feedback on 'problem' answers. If the students are given too much of the paper to 'get on with', the number of problem questions becomes too large, and students start to forget what the problems were. I would generally recommend no more than two pages from most exams as a *maximum*.

It is always amazing to onlookers to see just how quickly young, and even students with poor attainment, can become engrossed in this exercise. It is also extremely powerful as a method of finding out which areas of a topic are, or are not, fully understood by the students or, of course, which type of questions are, or are not, understood. Many teachers who tried this technique commented on how surprised they were that questions they expected the students to not have any problems allocating marks to would often be ones that caused arguments, whereas other questions that teachers expected to be 'tricky' would turn out to be readily agreed on by the students. As with verbal discussions (see chapter 2), the teacher can learn so much by simply listening to students grappling with incorrect answers or misunderstood concepts.

As an exercise, this takes *no more time* than the traditional 'going through the paper' but the benefits both for students and teacher are huge. I remember watching a Year 13 International Baccalaureate biology lesson in which the teacher, at my suggestion, tried this for the first time. One student, who would go on to gain a (top) grade seven and her place at Cambridge University, spoke to me during the process and said, 'In all my time doing science, I have never really thought about my answers before, other than if they were right or wrong. I have just realised that although I get most right, I tend to write about twice as much as I need to, mostly because I waffle so much. It's no wonder I always have to rush to finish an exam.' This extremely useful piece of self-learning that may well have proven crucial for her final grade, she had discovered after only *one* session of marking without a mark scheme!

Following the session, the papers should be taken away and the marking 'checked' by the teacher, which is a much quicker exercise than actually marking from scratch. The teacher should already be aware of which actual questions needed more careful examining, having listened to the debates on what should or should not gain marks, so those that had not proven difficult for the students to correctly mark can simply be ignored, and their pencil ticks used, when adding up the total score. This often makes marking time for the teacher *shorter*! However, what it always does, is ensure that the teacher focuses more on the answers that the students were less confident with, which is another fabulous benefit.

I have also found that students enjoyed marking their assessments like this so much that on occasions where it was not possible to do this, they would usually complain!

This technique has also been used in other subjects, including maths and PE, where staff similarly reported great success with it across a wide range of ages and abilities.

Revision resource tests

As with the first time I mentioned marking without a mark scheme to students, there was a similar reaction of total surprise the first time I suggested that an end of topic test in science would be done and that the students would be able to bring with them, *and use*, their revision resources. The students were convinced (perhaps not for the first time!) that their science teacher had gone mad! (This was a girls' grammar school, although the technique has since been very successfully adopted in various other secondary schools, at all ages and levels of attainment.) Without fail the students, when first being told of this, would state that, 'If we have our revision resources, obviously we will get everything right.' Clearly this was *not* the case.

This technique has been especially successful with KS4 and KS5. Students were allowed to bring with them all their relevant revision resources. When this technique was used with poor attaining students and those who were reluctant to produce their own revision resources, they were allowed to use a purchased revision guide. Students were *not* allowed to make use of classwork notes, nor their normal textbook. The whole point was that they would use the revision resource that they would eventually use to prepare for their final examinations.

One of the things this technique quickly flagged up, was that a number of students had not produced revision resources. Obviously this was dealt with, as would normally be the case, in line with the school's policy by the teacher. However, what was interesting was the invisible peer pressure of these situations. Students did not want to be seen as being 'different' from their peers, and if the other students were bringing in revision resources or revision guides, then they wanted to do so too. This was initially a surprising, but definitely hugely beneficial, aspect of this technique.

Another benefit that happened when doing these **revision resource tests**, over the course of a GCSE or A-level, was that the *quality* of revision resources produced by students noticeably improved. Again, this was seen not only in the grammar school, but also in other non-selective schools that adopted this technique. Never was this more telling than in Year 12. The girls at the grammar school were joined in Year 12 by boys from a neighbouring grammar school. The boys, being unused to revision resource tests, would almost always turn up at their first such test with a folded piece of paper with some odd notes scribbled on it. The girls, who had done similar tests at GCSE, would turn up with multiple pages of beautifully organised, colour-coordinated revision resources! It usually only took a couple of such tests for the boys to realise the standard of revision resources required and the benefits that they provided during the assessments. Usually by the end of the first term, the boys too would typically be arriving for their tests armed with well-organised, detailed revision resources.

Another obvious benefit that these revision resource tests produced was that students quickly came to realise that producing revision resources, is *not* the same as producing *useful* revision resources. Girls, in particular, tend to enjoy producing multi-coloured resources, often with as much information as possible, in as small a space as possible. However, they very quickly discovered that with such resources it is often far from easy to access particular facts or pieces of information in a short amount of time during a test. It soon dawns on these students that if they find it difficult to extract information from their resources, then actually *revising* from them will also be more difficult than they had hoped. In many instances, students discovered that 'less was more' with their revision resources, concentrating more on making key information stand out rather than on including as much detail as possible. Similarly, they realised that the presentation of the resources could greatly change how *useful* the resources actually were, often changing to use colour to code, or highlight information, rather than just for appeal.

In this way, revision resource tests undoubtedly improved not only the amount of revision resources that students were producing, but also their usefulness. So when the course came to its end the students already had all, or nearly all, of their revision resources not only produced, but in a format that they *knew* that they would be able to access quickly, and easily, for their final revision. Many, many students commented on how useful this was. Indeed, some students complained to teachers in other subjects for not using the same technique!

The final main benefit of revision resource tests was the improvement of students' examination technique. This was particularly true in biology, where students often complain that they 'don't know what the question wants them to do'. The revision resource tests highlighted the problems with examination skills – MARCKS – so that even when provided with the **K**nowledge in the form of revision resources, and even if these resources were extremely well done and usable, the students would still lose marks due to their lack of **C**larity or for failing to **R**ead the question properly, etc. This had a *huge* impact on the students, who quickly realised that 'more revision' was actually only *part* of the answer to improving their summative grades.

Finally, for any teacher wondering, revision resource test grades *were* used in *exactly* the same way as other summative assessment grades, on internal and external reports. Although the grade boundaries may have been different (usually higher) from other, more traditional summative tests, the range of grades produced still gave a very good indication of student progress. Nor were there any occasions, to my knowledge, of parents complaining about using revision resource test grades for reporting purposes.

In every respect revision resource tests were extremely successful at improving student *learning* and improving students' final grades.

The answer to the ultimate assessment question

Having asked many students the **ultimate assessment question** (see page 128) and received the familiar answers, it was very interesting to see how quickly, by adopting the various summative–formative linking techniques mentioned in this chapter, that the students' answers to this 'ultimate assessment' question altered. For example, at one parents' evening, when I said to my Year 12 biology group, 'So, you got a grade X this year. What are you going to do to ensure you get a (higher) grade next year?' *every* student answered by saying something such as: 'I have to improve the usability of my revision resources, and the **C**larity of my answers, by using more biological phrases' or 'I need to **R**ead the questions more carefully and take note of how many marks per question to make sure I get them all.' Such detailed understanding of *precisely* what was required for the students to improve their grades can only come about by adopting a completely different – more *formative* – attitude towards summative assessments, by both teachers *and students*.

As with all AfL improvements these did not happen overnight, but even from the outset the benefits were obvious. I remember thinking during that particular parents' evening, that if my headteacher could hear what was being said, perhaps she would have looked again at my salary! And can you just imagine if an Ofsted inspector were to ask your students 'how they could improve their grade' if the responses they received were as detailed as those described above?

Chapter 6
The proof of the pudding

6:1 Introduction – measuring success

During the original King's Project, Paul Black, Dylan Wiliam and the team used control groups and statistics to actually *measure* the improved performance of the effect of myself and my colleague using the various formative techniques we were experimenting with. At the time there were clear improvements in student performance, which were well documented, and became seminal findings, ultimately leading to the publication of *Working Inside the Black Box*.

However, detailed statistical analysis is not the only way to measure the success of classroom assessment in science lessons. I am sure that any teacher reading this book will readily agree that 'success' in the classroom is not always something that can be measured simply with a number. Therefore, what I wanted to show in this chapter is the wide range of responses from both teachers and students to the variety of ideas and techniques covered in the previous chapters. While by no means 'scientific', I honestly believe the wealth of feedback I and many other science teachers have had over the years, builds up a clear picture to the success of adopting this approach to teaching science.

I have already mentioned how when my colleague David and I first started introducing formative techniques into our teaching, many other members of our science department were keen to find out what we were doing and why. This came about not simply because David and I were unable to stop talking about what we were doing, but mainly because of the 'buzz' from students who were attending our lessons. 'In our science lessons we do...' was such a powerful first step in highlighting that there was definitely something positive about formative assessment in science.

The response of both other teachers and students to AfL has always been the main motivator that has driven me on. So, I have divided this chapter into two sections, looking at feedback and responses first from teachers and then from students. I have tried to include a few examples that will hopefully illustrate the impact that the various techniques and this approach to teaching have had on both of these groups.

Finally, just in case you were wondering, every single one of the quotes and examples below, are genuinely from teachers and students.

6:2 Teacher responses to AfL techniques

With teachers, I have deliberately tended to use quotes from more experienced teachers. This is not because I have not valued the feedback from younger or less experienced staff, but because it is the more experienced teachers who are inevitably more likely to be set in their ways when it comes to their teaching methods. I have discovered over the years that if the techniques and suggestions in this book impact on more experienced teachers, then changing approaches to teaching become much more achievable throughout the science department and across the school.

Teacher responses to 'planning for learning' (chapter 1)

I mentioned on pages 23-24, the response of an experienced head of maths to altering her learning objectives to make them more like success criteria and the dramatic effect that this small change had on her feedback from lesson observations, but even just changing the learning objectives to make them more 'success criteria-based' has produced other notable feedback from staff.

One experienced science teacher said that he was 'astounded by the difference that rewording the learning objectives had made to the students'. He went on to add that, 'It's the first time I have ever heard the students actually talking to each other about the learning objectives *during* the lesson. Which made me think about what I had actually been achieving, or more correctly not been achieving, with my old-style learning objectives.'

I could include many other examples of similar positive feedback from teachers here, but I feel that together with the head of maths feedback mentioned earlier, this clearly illustrates the typical 'wow' moment that I have often seen, or heard, when other teachers have first approached their lesson planning using a more learning-led approach.

When it comes to the *order* in which lessons are planned, most staff usually think that making the changes to put planning of their plenaries immediately after the planning of their learning objectives will make no difference at all. One such teacher was an experienced head of chemistry at the grammar school where I taught. Following on from a session of staff training where I had explained this 'different' way of *planning for learning*, he came to see me a few days later to say that he had 'given the idea a go', although he said that he had not been expecting anything different. He went on to add that, 'After teaching for so long, I really could not see why this small change in the order of my planning should matter, but I was shocked at how much better my lessons were – literally overnight.'

Following on from the same training session, a maths teacher in her final year before retirement came to see me and said how much she wished that 'somebody had shown me how to properly plan lessons before my final year. I tried your idea, and it was amazing. I couldn't believe that something, so simple, made such a difference to my lessons.'

It is interesting that the response of so many, usually experienced, teachers is one of shock or amazement that *no extra work* in their lesson planning can bring such noticeable differences to their teaching. I guess it is human nature to assume that if you have been doing something that does not cause outward problems, then what you are doing must, by default, be perfect.

With trainee staff, however, the responses to this approach to lesson planning tend to be different. One example was a student teacher who was on her first 10-week placement at my school. I mentored her during her stay and taught her how to 'plan for learning', as described in chapter 1. When she was observed by her visiting college lecturer one day, she came to me looking somewhat perplexed. It turned out that the lecturer had said that he had, 'rarely witnessed such an inexperienced teacher who had so clearly demonstrated, through a plenary, that the students had achieved each of their learning objectives, which showed exceptional planning.' She was surprised because, as she said, 'I had only planned the lesson in the same as I have done with all my others, I didn't do anything special.' The key point here is that to this new science teacher, planning for learning was all she had been practising. She was most surprised to discover that it was clearly not something her college lecturer was expecting.

Teacher responses to using more learning-led methods of questioning (chapter 2)

During the very early days of The King's College Project, when my colleague David and I were first trialling ideas for formative assessment techniques, one of the first things we tried was using longer wait times when asking a class a question during discussions. We both spoke at various department meetings and informal gatherings over coffee of how successful this 'improved thinking time' technique was. As mentioned earlier in the book, many of the young, keen science teachers wanted to try out all of our ideas. However, there were a couple of older, more cynical science staff members who showed no interest, or who would simply 'put down' anything that was said on the subject. One such colleague simply did not say anything at department meetings, and did not join any informal chats on what we were trialling. However, several weeks into the project, at one particular department meeting, David and I (along with the rest of the department) were both amazed when this particular member of staff suddenly spoke up. Out of nowhere, she suddenly said, 'It did make a difference.' At which point, everybody in the department looked at her. Realising she had to elaborate, she added, 'I tried leaving longer wait times after I asked questions to my Year 11 group, and it did make a difference. I noticed that more boys put hands up than normal.' There was a stunned silence in the meeting, and later David and I spoke about how if Paul Black, Dylan

Wiliam and the King's College team needed evidence that there was definitely 'something in this formative assessment stuff', they should have videoed our department meeting.

There have been many examples over the years where teachers have given all sorts of positive feedback following in-service training on how to make questioning more formative, but this very first response, from an ultra-cynical department colleague, still stands out as the ultimate confirmation of the way in which this technique impacts teachers.

One other piece of feedback on the subject of using more learning-focused questioning techniques came after I was observed by a student about to embark on a teacher training course. After my lesson he said, 'I was amazed by how many students actually joined in with your discussions. There can't have been more than a few who you didn't hear from. You use so many good ideas to get more of them involved.' Obviously, I couldn't resist, and so I replied, 'There were actually six who didn't say anything.' I had to hide my smile at his look of bewilderment. If you have read page 76, hopefully, this will make you smile too.

These two examples, I feel, summarise the type of responses from teachers on the subject of questioning and discussions. It has been notable over the years just how often teachers have agreed with me that this vital area of teaching had been almost totally neglected, at a practical level, during their own teacher training.

Teacher responses to using more formative methods of feedback (chapter 3)

Let's face it: most teachers find 'marking' a chore. I am sure there are not many who look forward to spending the evenings, weekends and holidays wading through pages of work and writing comments on them. I guarantee that you will not have to look far in a staffroom, or even in a science department meeting, to find teachers who complain about 'the time I waste marking, when the students are not even interested in my comments'.

Considering this, it is probably not surprising to learn that out of all the sections in this book, that it is the introduction of the ideas covered in the chapter on feedback that has always resulted in the most responses from teachers.

The initial response to the very first introduction of the **assessment stamp** (see page 96) was typical of any new initiative in a school, where most inexperienced staff were open to trying the new idea, and many of their more experienced colleagues responded with, 'Why do I need this? I have coped well without it for years.' What was interesting, however, was how quickly this attitude changed. Within only a few weeks, not only had these negative comments disappeared, but staff were beginning to talk about the impact of the new assessment stamp on their 'marking'. One such example was the head of physics who, after using the new assessment stamp for a few weeks, said, 'I am definitely spending less time marking now than I used to. My comments are so much more focused, and I don't waffle or repeat myself. But not only is it quicker, I have also noticed that the students seem to read and respond to my comments better. Talk about a win-win situation.' This type of response turned out to be typical.

The head of history also spoke to me about the impact of the assessment stamp after it had been implemented across the whole school. To assess the impact of the stamp he had carried out a departmental review of 'marking'. He said, 'I can't believe how quickly the assessment stamp has helped our department to have a much more *consistent* level of marking. When I did a book review last year, the quality of marking in our department varied hugely. This year there is much less inconsistency, and the quality across the department has really improved. I'm amazed how much difference the stamp has made.'

This was later echoed by a full-school assessment review, where consistency of feedback across the school was found to have improved enormously. After the review the headteacher said to me, 'The cost of the assessment stamps seemed a lot at first, and to be honest I was not convinced of success. However, I honestly can't think of anything else where we have spent a few hundred pounds more productively.'

I could fill this chapter with responses from teachers on the use of feedback techniques. I feel, however, that these examples summarise the general feedback I have received over the years, which have almost universally been positive.

Teacher responses to training students in peer and self-assessment (chapter 4)

The idea of having to continually train students to be able to peer or self-assess work usually comes as a total shock to most teachers. However, the realisation of the need to do this usually dawns on them very quickly, once they give it some thought. Typical feedback from teachers after experimenting with training their students (see chapter 4) would be, 'I always assumed that it was because the students just didn't care, or were too immature, that they did self/peer assessment so badly. But now it is obvious that they just didn't know how to do it properly.' This comment was made by a head of religious studies, in a secondary modern (non-selective) school.

Another memorable example of feedback on peer and self-assessment came from an experienced teacher who was also working part-time as a science adviser to other local schools. He showed me some of his GCSE group's books, in which he had tried to get students to peer assess work. Although the lesson had gone well, and understanding had obviously been good, the peer assessment was definitely awful – this was in a girls' grammar school, so literacy was clearly not an issue. The students had been writing statements such as, 'You have worked hard today' or 'You got everything right – well done.' After explaining how to structure the peer assessment comment, as described in chapter 4, several weeks later the teacher again showed me the books. This time they had comments such as, 'You clearly understand how synapses work, because you were able to explain how chemical transmitters helped in the process' or 'Your diagram on synapses helps to explain the role of chemical transmitters in how a synapse works.' My colleague said, 'It literally looks like these pieces of peer assessment are from another group of students – in fact, from a group several years older. I'm amazed at the difference this has made, in such a short time.' He was right; if anybody had seen the two examples of comments before and after training, they would never have thought that they were from the same students.

It is often the surprise that very good, experienced teachers have regarding the training of students in peer and self-assessment that is most notable and, as in the example above, how quickly students respond to these methods.

Teacher responses to using summative assessments in a more formative way (chapter 5)

When the MARCKS technique was first introduced as a method for feedback in science exams, it was initially trialled with a Year 10 exam. As always, some of the more experienced staff responded to being asked to try it out with less than positive attitudes. 'It's going to take me ages to mark a single set of papers,' or words to that effect, were common. However, after having used the technique for the first time during a review of how it went, the difference was amazing. All but one teacher said that it had not taken them any more time than usual to mark the papers. One said, 'Usually I write things like 'read the question' or 'check your calculations'. Being able to put a single letter, such as R or M, made marking it much quicker.' The general opinion was that for the *teacher* this type of feedback was definitely beneficial. However, the most telling comment came from a chemistry teacher, who was also a member of the Senior Leadership Team, and who had taught at the school for over 25 years. She said, 'In all the times that I have marked exams, this is the first time I have actually felt that I have given the students back anything that was actually worthwhile. And their response to the MARCKS stuff was amazing.'

Following on from the introduction of MARCKS and other formative techniques for improving summative assessments at a comprehensive school where I had delivered CPD, I was later contacted by the school's head of PE. Apparently, the science staff had been so impressed with how the students had responded to the new approach to their summative assessments, that they had been discussing it in the staffroom. As a consequence, the head of PE had discussed it at her department meeting, and the result was that the PE department had come up with their own list of basic skills to use in the same way with their summative assessments. In their case they spelled out not MARCKS, but SPORT. Unfortunately, I have long since lost the email that included all the details, but I seem to recall that the S was for 'scientific information', the R was for 'not reading the question properly' and the T for 'technique'. Although I cannot now recall all of these, it was noticeable that PE had realised that, as with science, they too had a few basic skills that tended to lose students marks on summative assessments.

As I mentioned earlier, these are only a small selection of the many, many comments from teachers I have received over the years, when they have been introduced to the various techniques covered in the earlier chapters of this book. It would be wrong of me to suggest that *every* comment I have received from colleagues has been positive. However, I can honestly say that such comments vastly outnumber any negative feedback. Of course, you do not have to take my word for any of this – feel free to try out the various techniques for yourself, and decide where you stand.

6:3 Student responses to AfL techniques

As much as it is reassuring to receive comments from colleagues regarding the use of classroom assessment techniques and methods for teaching, from my point of view, these have always paled into insignificance when set against comments from students. After all, it is *they* on whom the various techniques and ideas ultimately need to have a positive effect if any changes in teaching approach are to be worthwhile. As most teachers know all too well, there are always some students prepared to air their views on anything, and often everything, that a teacher is trying to do during a lesson, from the standard, 'This is boring' or 'I don't understand' to 'What's the point of this, anyway?' It is not surprising, therefore, that over the years since starting out on the King's College Project, there have been many occasions when students have 'had their say' on this different approach to teaching science. As with teaching colleagues, these student comments have also been overwhelmingly positive.

Student responses to learning-focused starters and plenaries (chapter 1)

I remember one of the first times I used the 'shared diagram' technique as a starter (see pages 33-34). It was with an A-level group and was being used to determine exactly what they had remembered about plant and animal cells from their GCSE work. At the end of the starter, one student said, 'Sir, that was such a good way of going back over the work on cells. I don't think that I would have been able to recall half of what I have just done, if we had just done some questions on it or something.' As most teachers will know, this is one of those moments worth burning the midnight oil for.

Another example of positive feedback about starters was when I heard a student speak to his friend while the group were moving back to their desks, after having completed a 'fishtail' activity on respiration (see pages 35-36). The lad said, 'That was really useful. I thought I had a good memory for this sort of stuff, until I saw what some other people remembered.' For me, this was another useful insight, as it confirmed my own thoughts on the activity in that it is not only about what students *can* recall, but what they *cannot*, from which they learn.

Another time, when we were doing my favourite ever plenary (see page 123) on the advice the students would give themselves on the lesson's work prior to an exam question on it, a girl said to me, 'I've not really thought about work like this before. My normal response would be to say, "make sure you remember everything", but actually, this has made me realise that just *remembering* it all, still might not be enough to get me a grade A answer. I have realised that knowing the processes is actually not as important as understanding the links between them.' This level of metacognition from a student is, I am sure you will agree, all too rare.

I could list many other similar examples under this section, but hopefully these are enough to illustrate that students not only *notice* when starters and plenaries are no longer 'bolt-ons' to their lessons, but genuinely appreciate their importance in developing their learning.

Student responses to more formative science discussions (chapter 2)

As I mentioned earlier, the project originally saw my colleague David and I both involved in the King's College Project and initially trying out various formative assessment techniques in our science lessons. The first of these techniques mostly concerned improving our questioning techniques with the use of more open-ended questions during class discussions, longer wait times, etc. At this stage in the project, we were only two teachers in the science department working on these techniques. Some time after our initial trials Christine Harrison, from the King's team, was interviewing some students in one of my science groups about class discussions in science, in order to gain the students' perspective on the new techniques. One student was speaking positively to Christine about how she liked discussions in my lessons, saying how so many students regularly joined in during science discussions, and how they really helped with learning. Christine then asked the student if this was specific to science this year, or if all science lessons were like this, or indeed, if other subjects were the same. The girl thought for a bit, then responded by saying, 'Mr Spenceley's discussions are really different from all my other subjects. I think the only other lessons I have ever had like this were with my previous science teacher.' Christine was obviously a little surprised at this and felt the success of discussions in science may have been long established at the school. She mentioned it to me later. Was it, Christine wondered, that my discussions were not really any different to what was long-time practice in the science department? However, when looking into the details of the girl who had made these comments, it turned out that in the past couple of weeks she had changed science groups, into my set, after previously being in David's group – her 'previous science teacher'. I am sure that Christine and the whole King's College team could not have wanted to have better confirmation of their early success.

Another example of the type of feedback from students that showed how much they noticed about the difference in more learning-focused discussions, rather than the more traditional science discussions, came during a parents' evening. I was congratulating a student on his input to the science discussions when the mother turned to her son and asked why it was that all other teachers said that the boy rarely joined in verbally in their lessons, whereas I was congratulating him on doing so. 'What makes science so special for you joining in?' she asked. The boy replied, 'Well, in science, *everybody* joins in, so I don't feel such a boff (short for 'boffin' – a student who was seen as too keen in the eyes of their peers!) and you can say stuff which isn't right, it doesn't matter.' The boy went on to add, 'And in science, we learn stuff when we are talking, which we use later, so you sort of have to join in.' The boy's mother said no more, and I simply sat there wishing that some of the other staff who taught the lad could have heard what he had to say. It was obvious that the lad had not only noticed the difference in style of his science discussions, but was able to clearly state how they benefited him. I added nothing to his explanation to his mum.

Over the years I have heard many other students say similar things to their peers, or to lesson observers such as student teachers, etc. Again, it is obvious that the students not only notice the difference in a more learning-focused discussion, but also appreciate its importance in their own learning.

Student responses to more formative written feedback (chapter 3)

I have already given some examples of responses to students to good-quality written feedback on their work, especially in regard to the effect on the students' response to the comment and any follow-up tasks that they have to complete (see chapter 3). One obvious notable response to this style of providing feedback that I particularly remember was when I had returned work to students marked using the assessment stamp (see page 96) on one of the first occasions I used it. At this point, it was still school policy to always put a grade on every piece of work, and in these early days, a grade was put alongside the assessment stamp comments. I vividly remember a conversation between two girls, which went as follows:

Girl 1: 'What did you get?'

Girl 2: 'It says I have to make sure that I use more scientific words in my answers. I always call things "it" or "they", rather than by their proper names.'

Girl 1: 'No, I meant what grade did you get?'

It was fascinating listening to this, as the second girl clearly did *not* see the grade as being the essential piece of feedback information she had been provided with, despite this being the common 'yard stick' by which *all* assessed work that she was used to receiving was normally measured. It was as a result of hearing several of these type of conversations by students that meant that I was later able to convince the headteacher to dispense with the rigid 'grade on all assessed work' policy, and move towards a comment-only feedback system that encouraged *learning*, rather than simply competition between students.

The assessment stamp was introduced to a variety of schools, and whenever it was first introduced, after it had been in use for a period, there would always be a reflection on its impact by asking a selection of students of different genders, ages and attainment levels to give their comments on the use of the stamp and the feedback that they had been receiving. Without fail, the feedback from students during these meetings was *always* positive, and in all schools the same words and phrases were used by students again and again to describe their thoughts: 'clarity', 'consistency', 'easy to understand', 'to the point', etc. However, from my point of view, the word that repeatedly came up during the student feedback sessions that I most appreciated was 'useful'. It may sound odd but if you have never tried it, try asking some students to use five or 10 words to summarise the feedback they receive on their work. You may be somewhat disappointed and disheartened to discover that 'useful' is rarely among their chosen list of words – unfortunately. Surely that will give you something to reflect on when you are next faced with a pile of work to 'mark'?

I have plenty of other examples to show how much students appreciate the use of a clear framework for providing formative feedback on their work, from across the age and ability range. These two examples, however, highlight the impact that these techniques have on something that is, after all, of huge importance to the students in developing their learning.

Student responses to peer and self-assessment training (chapter 4)

Although there have been comments on peer and self-assessment over the years, this is not an area where I have picked up a large number of comments from students. I am unsure why this is, perhaps because when done well, the process does not really stand out from any other aspect of teaching. Whatever the reason, I do not have comments to share here. This does *not* mean that I have only received negative comments that I did not want to include, but it does mean I am only using genuine examples from students throughout this section of this chapter, and I had no intention of inventing comments simply to make a point.

Student responses to the formative feedback on summative tests (chapter 5)

Again, I have already mentioned some examples of this in chapter 5 but this is the single biggest area where students have responded – almost always extremely positively – to the new techniques employed. I could easily write a whole chapter filled with examples of comments from students on this, but I will use a few to highlight the main themes. I can only assume that the reason for this level of response from the students is because summative assessments play such a huge part of their life in science, and this is such a totally different approach to providing feedback on such assessments.

With targeted revision techniques (see page 132-133) I have had many students with low attainment in science who have made comments, such as, 'I have never revised before. There has always seemed so much, that I just haven't bothered. But this way I have actually done some, and it *has* made a difference.' Whereas one boy, who had used traffic lights and targeted his 'amber' areas for revision after his exam, came to me to say, 'Sir, I have always revised, probably not as much as I should do, but when I was using the traffic lights, I realised I usually spend most time on the stuff I already know – I guess it's always seemed easy.' Clearly the technique had had an impact on him, which I would like to think would have been permanent, and perhaps even useful in other subjects too. I received many other similar comments from students, generally about the reduction in their workload, by adopting this more targeted approach to revision.

The task of having to provide an instant self-assessment on a test or exam has had some interesting responses from students. One of the most obvious, when this was first introduced in a mixed comprehensive, was that initially, in general, boys would overestimate their scores and girls would underestimate theirs. However, after becoming more used to the task, over time it was noticeable how often both genders became fairly accurate in their overall estimates – not necessarily with individual questions, but with the overall balance of the questions. Both genders quickly began to realise where they had done 'well' and 'not so well' on various parts of the summative assessment, which is obviously a key step in the students realising where further learning was required. One low-achieving boy summed this up very well when he said, 'I know I don't know everything in science, 'cause I'm not very good at it, but when I thought about it as soon as I had done the test, I realised that there were a few bits I knew. But I never know the maths or graph bits.' What is interesting here is that a student who lacked both scientific and literary ability was able to pinpoint at least one *specific* area of weakness in his science summative assessment. This was obviously much more useful to him than simply knowing that he had achieved a particular (almost certainly low) grade.

Some students did *not* enjoy making such an instant self-assessment immediately after completing a test. One girl said, 'The last thing I want to think about when I have finished a test is if I have got particular bits right or not.' However, such comments were definitely in the minority.

Fortunately, a more common response was one where an able student said that she 'found it really useful to complete the self-assessment, because sometimes when I am doing it I notice silly mistakes I have made, like putting the wrong units, or not rounding up an answer, like it asked for. Even though I used to check through my paper when I finished, I never used to notice these.' This highlights one benefit of immediate self-reflection. By 'forcing' the students to consider each question carefully, it also 'forces' them to look carefully at each individual answer, and not just 'flick through the pages' when doing their final 'check'.

Of all of the formative feedback techniques used with summative testing, undoubtedly, the one that made the largest impact on students was the use of MARCKS (see page 143). Although almost without fail, especially with lower achieving students, their **K**nowledge will see them lose most marks, what was always fascinating for the students was to see how often other skills also lost them marks. One low-achieving girl commented on this by saying, 'I am rubbish at learning science, so I always have lots of **K**s, because I can't remember all of the stuff, but I have noticed that I also lose a lot of **R** marks by not reading the questions carefully. I *can* read OK, so this is something that I am going to be more careful with in future, because obviously I can improve my score if I do.' Again, this clearly highlights a student identifying a *specific* area of weakness in their science test, rather than just their final grade. Importantly, she also saw that there *was* a possibility of improvement in her learning, despite her obvious lack of confidence in her own science ability.

With high-achieving students studying A-level biology, rather than **K**nowledge being the main problem area, it was often **R**eading of the questions that lost marks. One girl explained this very well when she said, 'I am so used to skimming through things when I read, that I tend to do the same with the exam questions. It's obvious that I need to read them more slowly, and carefully.' This turned out to be quite a common problem (as has been mentioned) with students working at the very top level of scientific ability, who would sometimes make 'silly' errors by missing key pieces of information in the – often long – introduction to A-level biology questions.

The other area where these same high-achieving students lost unnecessary marks was with their lack of **C**larity. So many times, when looking back through summative assessments using mark schemes, the students would say, 'That was what I meant,' despite the fact that they had not *specifically* used the biological phrase required by the examiner. This happened so frequently, that the word 'Clarity' became an everyday word in A-level biology lessons, where not only the teacher but also the students too, would pick up anything that was said that lacked Clarity. For my part, I have never accepted words such as, 'it', 'them' or 'they' from students, either verbally or in writing, as these words rarely appear on exam mark schemes. It was interesting to see that, as time went on, students too would 'call out' their peers over their Clarity if their peers used vague phrases when answering verbally.

One girl, who had repeatedly lost marks through her lack of clarity, decided to go back through every one of her past test and exam papers as part of her final revision, rewriting every answer, to be as clear and precise as possible. On receiving her A* in her final exam, she came to see me and said, 'I know it was improving my Clarity that got me the A* rather than an A. I was absolutely determined to nail it for these exams. Thank you for helping me with it.' With the thanks came a tie, pictured below, which she had had specially made for me. Somehow, I doubt if a student has ever had a tie made for a teacher with a grade on it!

I could go on here, but hopefully these examples will help to illustrate the impact that classroom assessment techniques can have on summative performance of students in science. I am certain beyond doubt that if science teachers want their students to achieve higher grades in exams – which I assume they all do – then helping those students to identify **how** to improve is more important than anything else.

6:4 The final proof of the pudding

All the kind feedback from colleagues, all the perceptive comments from students and everything else in this book would obviously be fairly meaningless if, at the end of the day, using these various techniques did not actually *improve student learning*, and as a result, their achievement in science. So, it would seem only fair to finish by looking at one very clear example of the impact of this approach to science teaching on exam results.

At my final teaching post in a high-achieving girls' grammar school, success at A-level was measured by the percentage of students who achieved an A*-B grade in their final exams. In 2010, the school average at A-level for this measure was 70%, with biology falling a little under average at 69%. In 2011, biology fell further behind the school average, and the headteacher asked me to 'make sure that all the science staff take on board all the work you have done on Assessment for Learning.' As a result, we introduced many of the techniques mentioned in this book over the next few years, so that by 2014, everything I have covered in this book was being used regularly by all GCSE and A-level science students. The following graph shows the impact of the new classroom assessment-focused approach on final A-level results in biology (my subject, which is why I have the details for this), compared with the overall school average, shown as a dotted line. This graph, I believe, really does show 'the proof of the pudding'. But please remember these are *not* figures, they are *actual students*, who really did have improved life chances as a result of their improved learning.

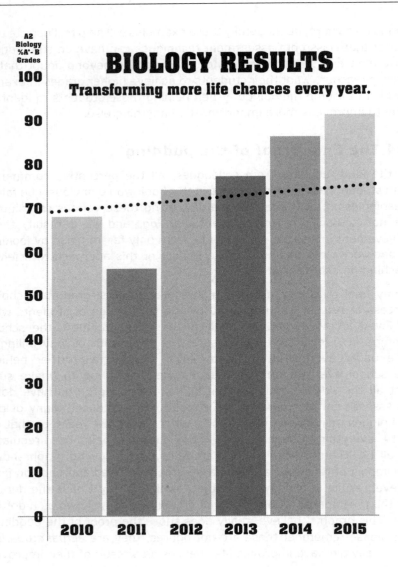

And finally...

In summary

The aim of this book was to make any science teacher – or prospective science teacher – reading it, stop and think about their teaching from a different perspective. I very much hope that if you have read it all up to here, that it has indeed *made you think*. If it had not been for Paul Black and the King's College team, I would never have been lucky enough to have been given the opportunity to reflect on my own science teaching. Hopefully, this book will act as a short cut through my 20 years of experience of Assessment for Learning in science, and in turn, it will inspire others to strive for new and improved ways in which to help their students to become better learners.

Thanks

I would like to thank everybody at John Catt Educational for all their efforts in producing this book. In particular to Alex Sharratt for having the bravery to publish the notes of a novice author. Thanks also to Jonathan Barnes for his role in coordinating the project. Finally, for all her help and advice with editing, and for dealing with the poor spelling and grammar of somebody unfortunate enough to have been educated in the 1960s, when both were considered unimportant, special thanks to Natasha Gladwell.

My thanks must also go to those people who have offered to read and provide feedback on early versions of the book, especially Christine Harrison, Shirley Clarke, Sue Swaffield, Niamh Spinola and Jenny Walsh.

I know how exceptionally busy they all are, and I greatly appreciate the time they gave and their encouragement.

I feel like the luckiest ever science teacher to have had so much support over the years, with all aspects of my work, and I would need another book to personally thank everybody. However, I do want to highlight some people who have made significant contributions, without which, this book would not even exist.

Firstly, and most notably, are Paul Black, Dylan Wiliam, Christine Harrison and all those involved in the King's Medway Oxfordshire Formative Assessment Project. Without them, I would have continued to be a 'hamster in a wheel' for the rest of my teaching, and I will never be able to thank them enough.

Both Christine and Dylan have also been very supportive when it came to me putting my ideas down in this book. My thanks must especially go to Dylan, for not only offering to write the foreword for the book, but also for acting as my primary editor and correcting many of my grammatical errors.

Many colleagues have helped and supported me along the way, not least David Tuffin, who started out on the King's College Project with me, and was with me throughout the first 10 years of development of formative assessment techniques in science. Although we then went our separate ways in terms of career paths, David and I have remained great friends and colleagues, and he has always been there to share thoughts or listen to ideas, on anything that helps to improve the learning of science by students. He also happens to be a truly outstanding science teacher.

Next, my thanks should go to all my colleagues in the science department at what the King's College Project referred to as 'Century Island School'. Here, all the earliest formative assessment ideas were trialled, to which the whole science department contributed so much in terms of feedback, support and encouragement. The enthusiasm of Mark Osborne, Gary Vyse, Vicki Anderson, Kathy Esmonde, Jenny Lucking, Doc White, James McCafferty and all the others who came and went, meant that they really were 'the dream team' to work with – superstars one and all.

Thanks too, to my headteacher at the time, Ray Robinson, for his amazing support of myself, David and the others involved in the King's

College Project, and later, for allowing David and I to present our ideas and findings to other schools and at conferences.

Finally, from my time at 'Century Island', I would like to thank Sue Swaffield, who was then the local authority adviser. Her support for the King's College Project, and for the work done thereafter by David and myself, was always superb.

At the Rochester Grammar School, I was lucky enough to have two of my former colleagues from the 'Century Island' to work alongside; Vicki and Kathy made establishing Assessment for Learning in science so much easier, and being such great science teachers, they provided lots of useful feedback. Vicki's contribution to the final MARCKS idea also cannot be overstated.

Thanks too, to Jon Sullivan who, as an AST and fellow biologist, was always willing to trial out new ideas, and offer his feedback and support. Also, my thanks go to Noel Sturt, who similarly offered help and support, and who played a big part in developing the Smart Revision Sheets, and the front covers of summative assessments. In the same way, Lara Osmotherly and Lucy Taylor were always incredibly positive about adopting, using and feeding back on the various techniques covered in this book.

Finally, at the Rochester Grammar School, my thanks to all the rest of the teachers in the science department and across the school, many of whom took the ideas into their own departments and provided all sorts of useful feedback.

I have been lucky enough to visit many other schools, in a variety of locations across the country and have spoken at many conferences in England and Scotland to colleagues. Whether speaking to large groups of teachers or just a few staff, on every occasion, fellow teaching colleagues have been positive and enthusiastic, which has always pushed me further.

I would also like to thank all those who have read through this book, whether you agree with the things in it or not. Either way I would love to hear from you, especially if you decide to trial any of the ideas mentioned. My contact details are at the end of this section.

My thanks must also go to my wife, who has not only provided large quantities of posters to promote the various ideas mentioned in this book, but who has supported, encouraged and simply been there for me, for over forty years.

Finally, and without a doubt, most importantly, I would like to thank every single student I have taught over the years; especially those who have had to put up with 'Sir' trialling yet another new idea. There have been groans about Clarity, moans about self-assessments and complaints about feedback, but these have always been in the minority, and far less than the complaints about my jokes! Above all, I have received hundreds, make that thousands, of positive bits of feedback from students about their work and progress in learning in science. Every single thing I have written about in this book, and every single aspect of my teaching, has ultimately been decided by and inspired by them.

If you would like to contact Paul Spenceley about this book in any way, please feel free to email **paulfspenceley@gmail.com**

Index